ASPECTS OF WAGNER

ASPECTS OF WAGNER

===

BRYAN MAGEE

===

Revised and enlarged edition

Oxford   New York

OXFORD UNIVERSITY PRESS

1988

Oxford University Press, Walton Street, Oxford OX2 6DP

Oxford New York Toronto
Delhi Bombay Calcutta Madras Karachi
Petaling Jaya Singapore Hong Kong Tokyo
Nairobi Dar es Salaam Cape Town
Melbourne Auckland
and associated companies in
Berlin Ibadan

Oxford is a trade mark of Oxford University Press

First published 1968 by Alan Ross
Second edition first published 1988 as an Oxford University Press paperback
and simultaneously in a hardback edition

British Library Cataloguing in Publication Data
Magee, Bryan
Aspects of Wagner.—2nd ed. rev. and enl.
1. Opera in German. Wagner, Richard,
1813–1883—Critical studies
I. Title
782.1' 092' 4
ISBN 0–19–217768–0
ISBN 0–19–284012–6 Pbk

Library of Congress Cataloging in Publication Data
Magee, Bryan.
Aspects of Wagner.
Includes index.
1. Wagner, Richard, 1813–1883—Criticism and
interpretation. I. Title.
ML410.W13M105   1988   782.1' 092' 4   88–9868
ISBN 0–19–217768–0
ISBN 0–19–284012–6 (pbk.)

Typeset by Cambrian Typesetters
Printed in Great Britain by
The Guernsey Press Co. Ltd.
Guernsey, Channel Islands

To Bernard Williams

PREFACE TO THE REVISED AND ENLARGED EDITION

NEW readers who see the word 'enlarged' applied to this edition may well think the earlier ones must have been short. So they were, consisting in effect of the first five chapters of the present volume. I have revised these once more, and added a sixth.

I am deeply grateful to David Miller for his reading of the manuscript, which resulted in many improvements. Any new errors that may have crept in are entirely mine.

January 1988   BRYAN MAGEE

CONTENTS

1. *Wagner's Theory of Opera*

Lohengrin, which for many years was the most often performed of Wagner's operas, was finished in 1847, when he was 34. From then until the age of 40, when he began the music for *The Ring*, he composed nothing at all—the only such gap in his creative life. What he did instead, having developed to its limits the form of German Romantic opera he had inherited, was to carry out a complete reappraisal of it. This was done, characteristically, in public, in a series of books, most of them written between 1848 and 1851. The most important of these were *The Work of Art of the Future* (1849), *Opera and Drama* (1850–1), and *A Message to my Friends* (1851). They embodied an entirely new theory of opera, which he then went on to realize in his remaining works: *The Ring*, *Tristan and Isolde*, *The Mastersingers*, and *Parsifal*.

This is a unique phenomenon. Here was a great artist theorizing about his art in volume after volume of published prose, and then going on to embody the theories in creative masterpieces. We should say it was all too self-conscious and synthetic, did not the works themselves refute this. Some writers have asserted that the practice is quite different from the theory and independent of it, but no one can seriously maintain this who has actually read the books, where over and over again practices to be found subsequently in Wagner's greatest works are elaborated in advance. It is true that he was later to change his overall view of opera in important respects, partly under the influence of Schopenhauer, but most of his detailed theories were then carried over and retained, to be realigned within the new framework. It is also true that at no time were his practices one hundred per cent faithful to his theoretical principles—whose ever are? The fact remains that to the end of his days his compositional techniques continued to embody many if not most of the theories expounded in those early writings. I cannot help suspecting that critics who deny this are tacitly and hopefully justifying themselves for not having read them. Wagner's theories are constantly being described as nonsense by people who do not know what they are.

I must say, though, that anyone who wants to avoid reading Wagner's prose has my sympathy. He writes like an autodidact, with flowery expressions, a vocabulary intended to impress, unnecessary abstractions, and elaborate sentence structures. (These faults are compounded in the nineteenth-century English translation by Ashton Ellis, *Richard Wagner's Prose Works*, in eight volumes: when Bernard Shaw called this 'a masterpiece of interpretation and an eminent addition to our literature' his usual critical acumen had been given a day off. In this book I have attempted my own translations.) One forms the conviction that the prose was improvised, poured out without forethought or discipline—that when Wagner embarked on each individual sentence he had no idea how it was going to end. Many passages are intolerably boring. Some do not mean anything at all. It always calls for sustained effort from the reader to pick out meaning in the cloud of words. Often one has to go on reading for several pages before beginning to descry what, like a solid figure emerging from a mist, it is he is saying.

No doubt there are many reasons for this, but I think the chief is that new things were beginning to form inside him that he was trying to articulate as a theoretical system when all the time their unconscious, autonomous development was towards works of art. In other words, I think that although his subsequent operas embodied most of his theories, and were given to the world after his theories, it is the theories that derive, so to speak, from the operas rather than the other way round. Something Wagner said many years later confirms this: the attitude of mind in which he had written those theoretical works had been, he said, an abnormal one because it had driven him 'to treat as an intellectual theory something that my creative intuition already had an assured grasp of'. Even allowing for probable exaggeration of his former assurance, it explains a fact that has puzzled many people, the fact that operas so deeply felt should incorporate pre-existing theories; and that the one to embody them most successfully, *Tristan*, should be the most passionately and spontaneously composed of all.

Wagner's central theory of what opera should be is interesting on many levels: for itself; as the most important contribution to the subject by any great composer; and for the light it throws on his works. One of the most fruitful and influential books on opera to be published in our half-century—*Opera as Drama* by Joseph Kerman, published in 1956—begins with the words: 'I make no apology for the Wagnerian title. This book is far from Wagnerian, but the point of view it develops is really the basic one celebrated by *Opera and Drama*, that astonishing volume of a hundred years ago . . .'

I shall try now to give a clear exposition of Wagner's theory. And because Wagner's writing is so little conducive to quotation I shall put it largely in my own words.

The highest point ever reached in human creative achievement was Greek tragedy. This is for five main reasons, which need to be considered together. First, it represented a successful combination of the arts—poetry, drama, costumes, mime, instrumental music, dance, song—and as such had greater scope and expressive powers than any of the arts alone. Second, it took its subject-matter from myth, which illuminates human experience to the depths and in universal terms. 'The unique thing about myth is that it is true for all time; and its content, no matter how terse or compact, is inexhaustible for every age.' Third, both the content and the occasion of performance had religious significance. But fourth, this was a religion of 'the purely human', a celebration of life, as in the marvellous chorus in the *Antigone* of Sophocles that begins:

> Numberless are the world's wonders, but none
> More wonderful than man . . .

And fifth, the entire community took part.

This art-form was ideal because it was all-embracing: its expressive means embraced all the arts, its subject matter embraced all human experience, and its audience embraced the whole population. It was the summation of living.

But with the passage of time it disintegrated. The arts all went their separate ways and developed alone—instrumental music without words, poetry without music, drama without either, and so on. In any case its available content dissolved when Greek humanism was superseded by Christianity, a religion that divided man against himself, teaching him to look on his body with shame, his emotions with suspicion, sensuality with fear, sexual love with feelings of guilt. This life, it taught, is a burden, this world a vale of tears, our endurance of which will be rewarded at death, which is the gateway to eternal bliss. In effect this religion was, as it was bound to be, anti-art. The alienation of man from his own nature, especially his emotional nature; the all-pervading hypocrisy to which this gave rise throughout the Christian era; the devaluation of life and the world and hence, inevitably, their wonderfulness; the conception of man as being not a god but a worm, and a guilty one at that; all this is profoundly at odds with the very nature and existence of art. Such a religion, based as it is on the celebration of death and on hostility to the emotions, repudiates both the creative impulse and its subject matter. Art is the celebration of life, and the exploration of life in all its aspects. If life is unimportant—merely a diminutive prelude to the real Life that is to begin with death—then art can be of only negligible importance too.

The long decline of art from the summit of the Greeks' achievement had reached rock bottom by the nineteenth century. From being a religious occasion in which the entire community took part theatrical performance had degenerated to the level of entertainment for tired businessmen and their wives. It was frivolous, often to the point of contentlessness, and such values as it embodied were those of the Christian-bourgeois society around it. The most frivolous, vulgar, socially exclusive, and contentless of all theatrical forms was opera. Its conventions were grotesque, its plots ridiculous, its libretti fatuous. Yet none of this was thought to matter, either by its audiences or its creators, for these things were there only to provide a framework for stage spectacle, catchy tunes, and vocal display by star singers. In spite of all this, though, opera was potentially the greatest of the arts, for it alone in the modern world could combine all the others in the way Greek tragedy had done. What was needed, therefore, was a revolution in opera that would turn it into the comprehensive art-form it was capable of becoming, in which all the resources of drama, poetry, instrumental music, song, acting, gesture, costumes, and scenery would once more combine in the theatrical presentation of myth to an audience of all the people. The subject matter of such works, though purely human, would be the deepest things in life. Far from being mere entertainment, therefore, they would be almost religious enactments.

This, in a nutshell, was the Wagnerian programme. It was not based just on the slogan 'Back to Greek tragedy', for it looked forward to a new and better way of doing what the Greeks had done—better, because it would draw on resources that the Greeks had not had. Shakespeare, 'a genius the like of which was never heard of', had developed poetic drama beyond anything the Greeks could have conceived. Beethoven had developed the expressive powers of music beyond the limits of speech altogether, even the speech of a Shakespeare. The artist of the future (no marks for guessing who) would combine the achievements of Shakespeare and Beethoven into a single art form, something that, on the analogy of poetic drama, could be called music drama.

How would music drama differ from existing opera and existing drama? Traditional drama depicts, for the most part, what goes on outside people, in particular what goes on *between* them. Its stuff is personal relationships. As for what goes on inside them, its chief concern here is with their motives. Dramatic development is a chain of cause and effect, one motivated action bringing about or conflicting with another, the whole adding up to a self-contained interlocking system that constitutes the plot. This requires that the forces that act on the characters be convincingly shown, and this in turn requires that they be placed in their social and political context, and their interaction with it articulated. The more motive is explored and displayed, the more 'political' the play has to be—the plays of Shakespeare conjure up whole courts and governments and armies, ruling classes, city states, feuding families, and the rest, with a vividness that would be unbelievable had he not done it, and always in terms of warmly alive individuals.

Music drama would be the opposite of this in almost every respect. It would be about the insides of the characters. It would be concerned with their emotions, not their motives. It would explore and articulate the ultimate reality of experience, what goes on in the heart and the soul. This had been made possible by Beethoven, who had developed in music the power to express inner reality in all its fullness, unfettered by the limitations of language with its dependence on the use of specific concepts and its permeation by the laws of logic. In this kind of drama the externals of plot and social relationships would be reduced to a minimum. Its chief requirement was for situations that remained unchanged long enough for the characters' full inner experience of them, and response to them, to be expressed. Myth was ideal for this, because it dealt in archetypal situations and because its universal validity, regardless of time and place, meant that the dramatist could almost dispense with a social and political context and present, as it were 'pure', the inner drama.

Music drama would also be the reverse of traditional opera, for in traditional opera the drama was merely a framework on which to hang the music—drama was the means, music the end— whereas the object of music drama was the presentation of archetypal situations *as experienced by the participants*, and to this dramatic end music was a means, albeit a uniquely expressive one.

Among the actual music dramas that Wagner then went on to write, *The Mastersingers* is an exception to these rules on many counts, owing to the fact that it was concerned with the one and only subject that he regarded as of fundamental importance yet 'political', namely the artist's relations to his art, and hence to tradition, and hence to society. Alone of the music dramas it is located in historical time and place—sixteenth-century Nuremberg—and has ordinary human beings as characters, one of whom, Hans Sachs, was a historical personage. Alone among Wagner's works it is a comedy, and the extroversion of its expressive language corresponds to this fact and to the 'political' subject: the verse lines are longer than in the previous works, they rhyme conventionally, and break up sometimes into stanzaic songs, while the music is altogether more diatonic, and in predominantly major keys. But the orchestra still performs the same function of articulating the existential drama, the flow of life and feeling inwardly experienced by the characters. The harmony with which inner and outer worlds are woven together creates a sense of well-being that pervades the whole work. The context is warmly and exclusively human, and yet the subject, though not mythical, had for Wagner a quasi-religious significance, and was intended to have such a significance for the audience. The audience being addressed is very much the 'folk', the whole community, which is itself represented in the opera.

What Wagner thought he had done above all else was develop an art-form that made possible the expression, and hence the experience, of unbounded feeling about specific things—what he called 'the emotionalizing of the intellect'. Beethoven, the first composer to proclaim his inner conflicts, had developed in music the power to articulate the inmost drama of the psyche, but because his expressive means were confined to those of absolute music he could give utterance only to generalized emotions; he could not be specific without resorting to words. His needs drove him in this direction, therefore, and in the last movement of his last symphony he introduced, for the first time, poetry. It was this combination of poetry and symphony that provided the take-off point for Wagner. He recognized that Beethoven's use of it had not been very successful, but he never ceased to acknowledge it as the starting point of his own work. When he laid the foundation stone of his own theatre at Bayreuth, on his fifty-ninth birthday, he marked the occasion with a performance of this work which was, in a sense, the foundation stone of his art. It was the *Choral Symphony* that had shown him that the symphony orchestra, with its language deeper than words but unspecific, could be combined with the human voice to provide a complex means of expression that used words and had all their advantages without being subject to their limitations. His own contribution was to bring this language into the theatre and use it as a means of dramatic expression with depths of utterance inaccessible to the Greeks, inaccessible even to Shakespeare.

Like Beethoven's music, Wagner's was symphonic, that is to say an organized structure consisting of themes and their development. But whereas in Beethoven's symphonies the course taken by the music—the exposition of the themes, their relative keys, their development, and their recapitulation—followed the requirements of sonata form, in Wagner's operas it followed the requirements of the drama. It did so on several levels at once, and technically the process was a complicated one. But a single aspect of it can be used by way of illustration to cast some light on the rest.

If, says Wagner—and this is his own illustration—he writes a line like *Liebe giebt Lust zum Leben* ('Love gives delight to living') the concepts involved are obviously congruent and therefore no change of key is called for. But if the line is *Liebe bringt Lust und Leid* ('Love brings delight and sorrow') then, since delight and sorrow are opposites, the music should modulate between them. What should happen is that the key in which the phrase begins on the word 'love' should remain the same through 'delight' and then change for the word 'sorrow'. The modulation must express the interrelationship of delight and sorrow in the state of love, and at the same time their difference; it must articulate their conditioning of each other. (This, said Wagner, was something words could not do, only music.) Now suppose the next line is *Doch in ihr Weh webt sie auch Wonnen* (which might be very freely translated: 'Yet even its pain gives us joy'). Then the key of 'sorrow' from the end of the previous line should be carried through as far as 'pain', because the emotional mood remains the same. But then the verb in this second line starts a shift of the mood back towards that of the first half of the previous line; therefore the music should begin to change key on 'gives', and on the word 'joy' should arrive back at the key of 'Love gives delight'.

Now this is just a very simple example involving two lines and two keys. In their long monologues or narratives Wagner's characters set all sorts of feelings and ideas and incidents and other characters in conflict, conjure up disparate memories, consider various alternatives, make decisions, change their minds; and the music modulates with them through multifarious and remote keys, giving subtlest musical expression to all these interrelationships, and above all revealing their underlying relationship to the primary key associated with the basic emotional mood of the scene.

Again, modulation is only one of the elements in music; Wagner absorbed all of them into the syntax of his dramatic language. The result was a symphonic web of infinite plasticity, moving freely in response to whatever was being done and said on the stage—which alone determined whether a new theme was introduced or an old one repeated, the guises they appeared in and the way they were developed; whether the music modulated or stayed in the same key, threw up a single melody or ramified into contrapuntal lines. This is what Wagner meant when he talked of putting music at the service of drama, of music being the means and drama the end. It is the opposite of opera as an excuse for music and spectacle—the traditional opera that, even if dramatically continuous, was always musically discontinuous, a series of self-contained 'numbers' of entirely unsymphonic character in which the orchestra was used chiefly as 'accompaniment'.

To listen to Wagner's music simply as music, without regard to the words or the drama, is to miss all this. It is to abstract the music from a very much larger but still single medium of expression—verbal-musical-dramatic—of which it is less than the whole. The music is so good that it is easy to do this and enjoy it, losing sight of what one misses. But how much one does miss astonishes those who, after half a lifetime of enjoying the music, for the first time study the texts and see the operas in performance.

Wagner's central theory is nourished by numberless tributary theories, each of which is argued out at length, either in context in one of the books or in a pamphlet or article to itself: how the mass of the people had come to be dissociated from art; the commercialization of culture; the history of opera and its decay; what political and social changes were needed before a comprehensive art form would again be possible; the strain of civilization; the relationship of the artist to society, and myth in its relation to both; symbolism; why speech alone is inadequate as a means of expression; the relationship between words and music; the development of symphonic music, and its application to drama; the different expressive powers not only of music and poetry but, within music, of harmony and melody, orchestra and voice. Some of the most illuminating discussions are among the most technical: the connection between key structure and poetic content; the reasons why the most appropriate verse form is characterized by short lines and alliteration.

On every one of these subjects, and many more, Wagner has interesting, important and frequently original things to say. On Beethoven he is outstandingly perceptive. His criticisms of traditional opera, though self-serving, are of lasting value. He had deep insight into the nature of symbolism (he was, of course, the acknowledged progenitor of the Symbolist Movement in French poetry). He had the most remarkable understanding, long before psychology or anthropology, of the psychic import of myth. He realized half a century before Freud that 'today we have only to interpret the Oedipus myth in a way that keeps faith with its essential meaning to get a coherent picture from it of the whole history of mankind . . .'. The essentials of modern psychology seem to be present, uncoordinated, in his writings.

Although Wagner's belief that the ultimate realities were those of inward experience led him to set a low value on political and social content in drama, he regarded widespread political changes in the world outside the theatre as necessary if art was again to occupy its rightful place as the focal point of man's life in society. So he was, as a young man, passionately interested in politics. Indeed he was an active revolutionary. All the theoretical works we have been considering were written in political exile, an exile that lasted for twelve years. They contain many echoes, in both ideas and phraseology, from the writings of Karl Marx up to and including *The Communist Manifesto*, which had just appeared in 1848. That Wagner had read Marx cannot be proved, but I think he must have done: he always had a vivid interest in whatever were the latest ideas; one of his closest political associates was Michael Bakunin, the most famous of anarchists, and it is scarcely credible that Bakunin should not have introduced Wagner to Marx when the two of them were active shoulder to shoulder as young revolutionaries; some of Wagner's writings have the surely unmistakable tone of someone who has recently read and been swept along by Marx. Be that as it may, Wagner's chief concern was not political economy but art—his real objection to existing society was that it was bad for art. It was his disgust with industrialism and the bourgeois hegemony, their alliance with the Christian Churches, and the way they degraded art to the level of entertainment, and turned most of the population into wage slaves cut off from everything that made life worth living, that drove him to take an active part in the Dresden rising of 1849 alongside Bakunin. The text of *The Ring*, which he wrote in the years immediately following, contains a great deal of political symbolism of a Liberal-cum-Marxist kind. (Bernard Shaw's book *The Perfect Wagnerite* is a detailed interpretation of it as a Marxist allegory.) By the time he came to write the music his views about the desirability of political symbolism in opera had changed. But the claim has often been made in print that the original model for Siegfried was Bakunin.

Viewed as a whole, Wagner's theories have major faults. One is their political *naïveté* and utopianism, characteristic of their time and place. Another is their romantic idealization of Greece—also characteristic of their time and place, having been given a dominant position in German thought by Lessing, Goethe, Schiller and Hölderlin, and then powerfully reinvigorated by Byron. A third is their historicism. The only way Wagner seems able to discuss anything is in historical terms. If he wants to advocate something, anything, he has to demonstrate that it once existed, describe how it worked, account for its decline, and then call for a return to it. This means that three-quarters of any argument from his pen is likely to be clothed in bogus history. To some subsequent critics the arguments have been not merely clothed but hidden—these critics have been under the illusion that when they had refuted the history they had destroyed the argument. This is not so. An argument can be illuminating, and its conclusion valid, even though the historical terms in which it is couched are inaccurate.

A more serious, if more elusive, objection is that there is something passive about it all—and also something solipsistic, the two being related. By filleting drama of motive and presenting it almost entirely in terms of emotional response Wagner shows things acting on people but not people acting on things. Their feelings in relation to situations and each other are poured out in unparalleled fullness, but this very fact means that the situation itself, or the relationship, is somehow 'given'. We see the characters almost entirely from the inside—very little as active in the world, assuming control of situations and changing them, precipitating events. The only kind of responsibility they ever seem to take is the passive one of acknowledging necessity. Wagner's recipe is for a drama that consists not of actions but of reactions. His characters are subjects only of feeling; of action they are always the objects. One can go even further and say that his main characters are victims: Tristan and Isolde obviously so, but also Wotan, who, in spite of being ruler of the Gods, is from the very beginning of *The Ring* at the mercy of forces he is powerless to control, and in the end he and all the gods are destroyed by them. Siegfried, though supposed to be the supreme hero, never at any time understands his situation and is always the puppet of his own ignorance, which in the end destroys him. Wagner's last opera, *Parsifal*, passes beyond even this degree of emotional passivity and concerns itself with total renunciation.

Solipsism is suggested by the fact that reality for Wagner is always to be found in the psyche, not in the external world. Inner emotion is so overwhelmingly experienced that everything else, including other people, has only a shadowy existence on its periphery. Wagner's characters do not seem really to relate to each other: the being of each is, as it were, a sphere of passionate feeling that reveals its interior to the audience but only its surface to the other characters. It has been said of *The Ring* that in the deepest sense there is only one character, the different 'characters' being aspects of a single personality, so that the work is a portrait of the psyche as well as a depiction of the world.

But for all its shortcomings Wagner's theory was the first to seize on the truth about the place of great music in opera, and its relationship to the drama; and it is still, after nearly a century and a half, at the centre of opera theory in general. It even has significance beyond opera: for instance it illuminates the function of poetry in Shakespeare's plays. Directly or indirectly it informs most serious discussion of the drama today. And its effect on the world of music would be hard to overestimate. As Edward J. Dent wrote in his book *Opera*: 'Wagner, through his writings and through his own personal influence, has converted the musical world, or a good part of it, to something like a new outlook on music in general. It may be be that he was mistaken in supposing that the modern world could ever recover the attitude of ancient Greece to the religious aspect of musical drama, but he certainly induced it to take music, and especially opera, far more seriously than it had ever done before.'

2. *Jews—Not Least in Music*

SINCE Darwin three people have produced theories about man and his environment that in depth, originality, and scope are equal to almost any before them—Marx, Freud, and Einstein. The theories are not compatible, but each is a creative achievement of the highest order, and their influence has been immense. Marx, in fact, has had more influence in less time than anyone else in history: within a mere seventy years of his death a third of the human race was living under governments that called themselves by his name. The intellectual achievement of Einstein is more impressive, and may prove in the end to be as important in its practical application, if only because it made possible the hydrogen bomb. As for Freud, he has done more to extend our vision inward, into ourselves, than anyone else; doing his work required unimaginable courage. All three, I think, must be ranked among the greatest of the world's creative geniuses.

And all three were Jews. This fact is remarkable for many reasons. One is that there had been only one Jew of comparable achievement, Spinoza, in the previous eighteen hundred years. Another is that, in spite of that, those three pioneered a Jewish renaissance of almost incredible proportions. Jewish philosophers since Marx include Bergson, Husserl, Wittgenstein, and Popper. Many of the famous psychoanalysts apart from Freud have been Jews, and in the sciences not only Einstein but Nobel Prize winners so numerous it would be tedious to list them. All this is doubly amazing when one remembers that the total number of Jews in the world is only about thirteen million—the population of Greater London.

In no field has their contribution been more outstanding than in music. Mahler was Jewish, as were Schoenberg and most of his famous pupils. The greatest instrumentalists of this century have been Jews. Even if one forgets Kreisler, Schnabel, and all the other great dead, and considers only the living, the best violinists are nearly all Jews—Menuhin, Stern, Milstein, Zukerman, Perlman, Gidon Kremer, Schlomo Mintz, Ida Haendel, and Miriam Fried. Jewish pianists include Horowitz, Serkin, Berman, Perahia, Ax, Barenboim, Annie Fischer, Rosalyn Tureck, Clara Haskil, Radu Lupu, Andras Schiff, Gary Graffman, and Shura Cherkassky. The conductors include Leonard Bernstein, Solti, Dorati, Levine, Leinsdorf, Previn, and Maazel. These lists, themselves grossly incomplete, cannot be matched by the 99½ per cent of the human race who are not Jews. If anyone wants to tell me this is coincidence my reply is that this is simply not credible. The intellectual and artistic output of Jews in this century relative to their numbers is a phenomenon for which I can think of few parallels in history since the Athens of five centuries before Christ. It is something that calls for explanation.

In fact there are two questions requiring an answer, each of which helps to set the other. First, why since the ancient world did Jews produce scarcely any creative work of the front rank until the nineteenth century? Second, why did there then follow this amazing harvest of achievement? Jews tend naturally to be more excited by the second question than the first. I have often heard them discuss it, and often discussed it with them. The trouble with the answers they most commonly produce is that they fail to accommodate the facts behind the first question.

One explanation, offered with extreme reluctance to a non-Jew (and for that reason, I am sure, more commonly believed than expressed), is that Jews are specially gifted in some innate way. But if that were so, why did they produce only one truly original genius in eighteen hundred years? Serious evidence is altogether against the idea that Jews are cleverer than others. Some who think it are really just reformulating the ancient doctrine of the 'chosen people' in terms of genetics; but there is not a scrap of genetic evidence for it. In the first place, the Jewish people do not constitute a gene pool, and are in that sense not a race at all. But even leaving that fact aside, German and American racists have tried hard in our century to produce scientific evidence for this kind of difference between races, and always failed. Jews, of all people, ought by now to be immune to Master Race theories. But perhaps that is asking too much of human nature. One's natural reaction to disparagement is to assert one's special value, and centuries of persecution can only have given the Chosen People doctrine added appeal. Nevertheless the belief by people of any race that they are inherently superior is beneath respect, and I have no hesitation in saying of this one, as of the others, that it is superstitious, false, and nasty. Most Jews, I am sure, do not believe it.

The explanation most commonly offered is that the cultural distinction of modern Jewry is due to its unique religious and intellectual tradition. But what this implies is the exact opposite of the truth. For it is only Jews who have escaped from their religious and intellectual tradition who have achieved greatness. Every single Jew I can think of who has reached the highest levels of attainment in the modern era has repudiated Judaism: Spinoza, Heine, Mendelssohn, Marx, Disraeli, Freud, Mahler, Einstein, Trotsky, Kafka, Wittgenstein, Schoenberg.[1] It seems, rather, that freedom from that most tribal, observance-ridden and past-oriented of religions is a precondition of true and deep originality.

Here we come to what seems to me the right explanation—and one that answers the first as well as the second of our two questions. Originality in fundamentals is inimical to any closed, authoritarian culture, because such cultures do not and cannot allow their basic assumptions to be questioned. The two greatest moralists there have ever been, Socrates and Jesus, were executed for doing precisely this. Only in comparative freedom—or at least

---

[1] Schoenberg returned publicly to the faith in 1933, but made it clear that this was not a religious conversion but a declaration of solidarity with the Jews in face of Nazi persecution.

when authority has been on the defensive—has individual creativeness flourished: in ancient Greece, the Renaissance, Protestant Europe, or the rest of Europe since the dawn of liberal thought. Authoritarian cultures—ancient Rome, classical China and India, medieval Christendom, contemporary Communism— have been by comparison barren. Of course they have had their brilliant lawgivers, scholars, theologians, establishment artists and so on *within the system*, but any man who denied the basic assumptions of the system itself was crushed—in most cases tortured and killed. In such circumstances radical innovation is impossible.

The great flowering of European drama, poetry, science, mathematics, philosophy, music, began with the emancipation of these activities from the Church. Not surprisingly it took two or three generations to reach full growth. So the peak came in the seventeenth century (though music, as always, was behind the others—just as, later, the high point of Romanticism in music came when the Romantic Movement in literature was already spent). There could have been no question of its happening within the Church. Some of the greatest geniuses of all, like Copernicus and Galileo, had their work officially condemned by the Church. The Inquisition that tried Galileo had thousands of less eminent intellectuals imprisoned, tortured, or executed. In Italy scientific work was stamped out altogether and did not revive for generations.

But in all this the Jews had little part—except in Spain, where they were treated in a way that foreshadowed the Nazis. Over most of Europe they were still living in a closed religious culture of their own, where they were condemned to remain until the ghettos were opened. The banning of instrumental music and graven images from the Synagogue meant that within that culture the development of the non-literary arts was just as impossible as the development of science. And when the ghettos were finally opened the Jews had a parallel renaissance of their own, with all the same broad features: the lapse of two or three generations between emancipation and the peak of achievement;

the dissociation of the greatest creative geniuses from the closed religious and intellectual tradition; the lifelong struggle against institutional prejudice and personal resentment—and, before the end, murder on an enormous scale, highly organized and state-supported.

If this explanation is the right one the Jewish renaissance was a once-for-all phenomenon—it can neither continue nor happen again. As time goes by the difference between Jews and non-Jews is bound to diminish. Now that most Jews, like most other Westerners, have abandoned religion the chief thing that gives them any active sense of being Jewish is anti-Semitism, above all the recent attempt to murder them all. Orthodox Jews dread and hate integration, but they are a minority, and now that the taboo on intermarriage has weakened for all but a few it is bound to happen to most Jews in the long run.

And what, it may be asked, has all this to do with Wagner? The answer is that he was the first person to see any of it—a small part, perhaps, but as much as it was possible for anyone in the nineteenth century to see, and more than anyone else in that century saw. And because of his anti-Semitism he has never been given credit for it. The Jewish renaissance has happened almost entirely since his day, and he did not foresee it, but he did regard the fact that there had been no really great Jewish composers up to his time as something requiring explanation. The explanation he offered was almost unbelievably original, and largely correct. The key document is an article he published in 1850 called 'Das Judentum in der Musik' ('Judaism in Music'). Its central argument is as follows.

A really great creative artist is one who, in freely expressing his own fantasies, needs, aspirations, and conflicts, articulates those of a whole society. This is made possible by the fact that, through his earliest relationships, mother tongue, upbringing, and all his first experience of life, the cultural heritage on which he has entered at birth is woven into the whole fabric of his personality. He has a thousand roots in it of which he is unaware, nourishing him below the level of consciousness, so that when he speaks for himself he quite unconsciously speaks for others. Now in Wagner's time it was impossible for a Jewish artist to be in this position. The ghettos of Western Europe had only begun to be opened in the wake of the French Revolution, and their abolition was going on throughout the nineteenth century. The Jewish composers of Wagner's day were among the very first emancipated Jews, pastless in the society in which they were living and working. They spoke its language with, literally, a foreign accent. In composing its music—including, quite often, Church music— they were turning their backs on a distinctive and entirely different musical tradition of their own. So their art could not possibly be 'the conscious and proclaimed unconscious', which Wagner believed all great art to be. It could only be synthesized at the upper levels of the personality. In fact its articulated content could originate no deeper than the composer's conscious intentions. So however great his gifts it could only be shallow by the standards of great art. 'Mendelssohn', Wagner wrote, 'has shown us that a Jew can have the richest abundance of specific talents, be a man of the broadest yet most refined culture, of the loftiest, most impeccable integrity, and yet not be able—not even once, with the help of all these qualities—to produce in us that deep, heart-seizing, soul-searching experience that we expect from art.'

One does not need to share Wagner's view of Mendelssohn, who came from a Christianized and highly assimilated family, to see that his argument is substantially correct. The obvious thing about it that Wagner failed to see is that of its very nature it relates to a transition period, during which its application was bound to diminish as the descendants of emancipated Jews became more and more absorbed into society. On the basis of his own argument he ought to have expected great Jewish composers to emerge in the future. Indeed, when they did emerge in the persons of Mahler and Schoenberg his argument illuminated something important about them. (Neither of them, incidentally, held Wagner's anti-Semitism against him; they both idolized him.) Both men were alienated from two cultures—each rejected the Jewish religion yet was a lifelong victim of anti-Semitism—and the music of both gave full expression to their personal and artistic isolation, including even its neurotic aspects.

What was happening then, and has been happening since, is that while with the passage of generations Jews were integrating with the Western cultural tradition, that tradition was disintegrating to meet them half-way. The atomization of society, the increase in pace of change and hence problems of adjustment, the consequent rootlessness of the individual, his alienation from himself, from society, and from the past of both—these have become major themes of the culture of our time. Our age is characterized by superwars, the mass migration of entire populations, the scattering of dozens of millions of individual refugees, and by genocide. With every one of these things Jews are likely to be identified, and emotionally involved, more deeply than other people. At last they are in a position unconsciously to articulate the deepest concerns of the age they live in. The Jew has become the archetypal modern man. But this is only another way of saying that the rest of us are now almost as badly off as the Jews—which culturally speaking is true. And this is another reason for believing that we are now in the final stage before integration.

The degree of Wagner's originality in this, as in so many things, is almost bewildering. As usual he was offering explanations for what other people had not even noticed. But the trouble, again as usual, is that what was marvellous about his contribution was commingled with what was repellent to such an extent that it got overlooked and rejected along with the rest. In this case the argument I have salvaged from his anti-Semitic writings is the baby thrown out with the bathwater. The bathwater was foul, just the same.

Wagner's anti-Semitism is strikingly similar in its personal origins to Hitler's. The worst period of deprivation and humiliation he ever had to suffer was the two and a half years during which he tried and failed to establish himself in Paris, which was then the world capital of opera, at a time when the roost was ruled by Meyerbeer, a Jew, and the next figure to him was Halévy, also a Jew. It came close to breaking his spirit. His very real fears found expression in a short story he wrote about a young German composer dying in Paris in neglect, poverty, and despair. Even in its duration the period of his mortification was roughly the same as Hitler's in the Vienna doss-house. Both men were the sons of petty officials, both were megalomaniac, and in both of them the experience of being brought to the edge of starvation by society's total disregard of them seems to have activated a sense of persecution that bordered on paranoia, cast 'the Jews' as the villains, and became a mad hatred that never died.

Wagner—ferociously conscious of his neglected genius, and utterly destitute—hated the works whose popular acceptance barred the way to his own. He saw them as gimcrack and fraudulent, which they were. He hated them all the more because in desperation he had succumbed to the temptation to write a work like them. ' "Grand Opera" stood there before me in all its scenic and musical pomp, its emotionalism, its striking effects, its sheer musical bulk. And the object of my artistic ambition became not just to copy it but to outdo it with reckless prodigality on all fronts.' So he wrote *Rienzi*, which von Bülow once described as Meyerbeer's best opera. The canon Wagner laid down in later life begins with the work he wrote after that, *The Flying Dutchman*. *Rienzi* has never been presented at Bayreuth to this day.

Wagner attributed all that was meretricious in Paris opera to the Jewishness of its composers. 'Of necessity what comes out of attempts by Jews to make art must have the property of coldness, of non-involvement, to the point of being trivial and absurd. We are forced to categorize the Jewish period in modern music as the period of consummate uncreativeness—stagnation run to seed.' Jewish music not only did but was bound to cultivate the surface qualities of attractiveness, technical skill, facility, fluency, charm, glitter, surprise, the striking effect. It was a succession of effects in the bad sense, 'effects without causes'. This was why it found its natural expression in the theatre of unmotivated spectacle—

Grand Opera. To write works of this kind was to make use of art as a mere means—a means of entertainment, a means of giving pleasure and getting to be liked, a means of achieving status, money, fame. For Jews it was a means of making their way in an alien society. 'Like all the Parisian composers of our day Halévy burned with enthusiasm for his art for just as long as he needed it to help him scale the heights of success. Once this was done and he had entered the ranks of privileged and lionized composers he cared nothing beyond turning out operas and getting paid for them. In Paris fame is everything, the artist's delight—and his destruction.' The first eight words of this quotation betray Wagner's double standard in the very act of trying to dissemble it. Gentile or Jew, nearly all artists who have been famous in their day and subsequently disregarded have been people who used their art to please others and win social and financial success for themselves. And it is a wry fact that of all the really great composers the least indifferent to money and fame was Wagner. However, after *Rienzi* he never again compromised his work to attain them. Never again did he attempt to use his art as a means to other ends. His view became that the world owed him a living as of right, in return for the works that he gave to the world. (It is ironical to reflect on the money and fame that have since been made out of these works by other people.)

In Wagner's defence it can more substantially be said that his central argument was correct, and decades ahead of its time; that it illuminates many side issues; that he acknowledged the eminence of Jewish intellectuals, as distinct from creative artists; and that he attacked the Christian tradition (see pages 5–7) as much as he attacked Judaism. Against this it has to be said that although the validity of an argument is unaffected by the motives of the person who uses it, it is still a fact that Wagner's motives in this case were twisted; that what is true in his argument could have been advanced without anti-Semitism, which was therefore superfluous even from his own point of view; and that his attacks on Christianity never had the same personalized venom as his attacks on Judaism.

The authority that most people erroneously suppose genius to confer has enabled Wagner's anti-Semitism to do terrible harm. Quite apart from anything else, Hitler made use of it. So there is poetic justice, albeit neither logic nor justification, in the fact that among the people who have been most damaged by it is Wagner himself.

3. *Wagnerolatry*

'WE recently had a very serious conversation on the subject of Richard Wagner', Pierre Louÿs wrote to Debussy; 'I merely stated that Wagner was the greatest man who had ever existed, and I went no further. I didn't say that he was God himself, though indeed I may have thought something of the sort.'

The worship of Wagner by people of all kinds, including some who were themselves possessed of creative ability of the highest order, and in fields quite different from music, is something unique in the history of our culture. 'Wagner's art was the great passion of Nietzsche's life', Thomas Mann wrote; 'He loved it as did Baudelaire, the poet of the *Fleurs du Mal*, of whom it is told that in the agony, the paralysis and the clouded mind of his last days he smiled with pleasure when he heard Wagner's name.' Of himself Mann wrote: 'My passion for the Wagnerian enchantment has accompanied my life ever since I was first conscious of it and began to make it my own and penetrate it with my understanding. All that I owe to him, of enjoyment and instruction, I can never forget: the hours of deep and single bliss in the midst of the theatre throngs, hours of nervous and intellectual transport and rapture, perceptions of great and moving import, such as only this art vouchsafes.' Commenting on this a few years later in the light of the misappropriation of Wagner by the Nazis he said: 'The words express an admiration that has never been diminished, no, not even come near to being, or ever could be, by any scepticism or any unfriendly usage to which the great object of it may offer a handle.' And then, later still, he described Wagner's work as 'a perfectly unique eruption of talent and genius; the achievement, at once deeply serious and completely ravishing, of a magician . . .'

One of the many extraordinary aspects of this extraordinary phenomenon is that Wagner was frequently worshipped not only in his works but in his person. King Ludwig II of Bavaria wrote to him: 'I can only adore you, only praise the power that led you to me. More clearly and ever more clearly do I feel that I cannot reward you as you deserve: all I can ever do for you can be no better than stammered thanks. An earthly being cannot requite a divine spirit.' If this were the only example we should write it off as a homosexual love letter but, incredibly, it was not at all uncommon for Wagner's friends to speak of him in this way. For instance Hans von Bülow, whose wife was later to bear three illegitimate children to Wagner and then marry him, talked of 'this glorious, unique man whom one must venerate like a god'.

Wagner's great enemy Hanslick—the critic so spitefully caricatured as Beckmesser in *The Mastersingers*—wrote in his autobiography: 'He exercised an incomprehensible magic in order to make friends, and to retain them; friends who sacrificed themselves for him, and, three times offended, came three times back to him again. The more ingratitude they received from Wagner, the more zealously they thought it their duty to work for him. The hypnotic power that he everywhere exerted, not merely by his music but by his personality, overbearing all opposition and bending everyone to his will, is enough to stamp him as one of the most remarkable of phenomena, a marvel of energy and endowment.'

One such friend, a now largely forgotten composer called Felix Draeseke, consoled another with these words: 'At present it is not exactly agreeable to have relations with him. Later, however, in another thirty or forty years, we shall be envied by all the world, for a phenomenon like him is something so gigantic that after his death it will become ever greater and greater, particularly as then the great image of the man will no longer be disfigured by any counter-considerations.'

He was right. Wagner was idolized after his death by people of all kinds: composers as disparate as Debussy and Mahler (who once said that in music there was only Beethoven and Wagner 'and after them, nobody'); by people famous for their irony and detachment, like Thomas Mann, or for their iconoclasm, like Bernard Shaw—who once wrote that even at performances whose incompetence beggared all powers of description, even his, 'most of us are at present so helplessly under the spell of *The Ring*'s greatness that we can do nothing but go raving about the theatre between the acts in ecstasies of deluded admiration'. Wagner Societies, founded in the composer's lifetime, flourished in many parts of the world. The number of books and articles written about him, which had reached the ten thousand mark before his death, overtook those about any other human being except Jesus and Napoleon. The religious language that had been used of his person continued to be used of his work: people talked of being 'converted' to his music, of 'making the pilgrimage' to Bayreuth —and were derided by others as 'fanatics'. Many indeed, like the composer Chabrier, cheerfully described themselves as fanatics.

The phenomenon has continued ever since, and we are all familiar with it. The devotion aroused in some people by Wagner's music is different in kind from that aroused by any other composer's. It is like being in love: a kind of madness, a kind of worship, an irrational commitment yet abandonment that, among other things, dissolves the critical faculty.

The equal and opposite reaction is just as familiar: the militant advocacy is equalled by a militant dislike. Wagner in his lifetime had more, and more bitter, personal enemies than any great composer has ever had, and his music can provoke a hostility not merely greater than any other's but, again, different in kind. People who would consider it silly to condemn the music of any comparably famous composer as 'bad' if the word were meant aesthetically, and meaningless if it were meant morally, do not hesitate to apply it to Wagner's in both senses. His music is denounced, as is no other, in moral terms: it is 'immoral', 'corrupting', 'poisonous', 'degenerate'. The notion that there is something inherently evil in it, a notion as old as the music itself, received its greatest boost from Hitler's worship of Wagner, and the composer's subsequent association, long after his death, with Nazism. To this day there are many people who feel there is something fascist about his music.

Here, then, we have a music that gets at people—not everyone, of course, but a remarkable number—in a unique way: gets under their skins, stirs passions that no other music touches, and draws reactions that, whether favourable or unfavourable, are essentially immoderate. 'Prejudice', said the fifth edition of *Grove's Dictionary of Music*, 'affects judgement of Wagner more than that of almost any other composer.' This fact has been notorious now for over a hundred years, but it has never, so far as I know, been explained. Yet I think it can be explained.

The key is this: Wagner gives expression to things that in the rest of us, and in the rest of art, are unconscious because they are repressed. Modern psychology has familiarized us with the idea—and convinced most of us of its truth—that in the process of growing up and developing independent personalities, and learning to live in society, we have to subordinate some of our most powerful instinctual desires, especially erotic and aggressive ones—for instance passionate sexual feelings towards parents and siblings, or the urge to attack and destroy those on whom we are emotionally dependent—so that these are driven underground, below the level of consciousness, and kept there at the cost of some strain, as a result of which they remain charged with a high emotional voltage. Most of the really important taboos in our society, such as the incest taboo, relate to them. This repression, this inner conflict, is inseparable from living, and is part of the personality of each one of us. I believe that it is from, and to, this level of the personality that Wagner's music speaks.

I cannot prove this, because the emotional content of music is not expressible in words, but from what *is* expressed in words— the texts of the operas and, quite separately, Wagner's prose writings—evidence rises up in abundance to support it. Let us look first at the operas. Their subject matter is, to a remarkable degree, the subject matter of depth psychology. Even today audiences would be shocked if the first act of a new drama were to consist of a prolonged, passionate love scene between brother and sister which culminated in sexual intercourse as soon as the curtain was down. Yet this is the first act of *Die Walküre*. And in the second act it is openly and explicitly approved. Wotan says

> What wrong
> Did these two do
> When spring united them in love?

And when Fricka (who, let us not forget, is the goddess of marriage) cries out

> My heart shudders,
> My brain reels;
> Marital intercourse
> Between brother and sister!
> When did anyone live to see it:
> Brother and sister *physically* lovers?

Wotan replies:

> You have lived to see it today.
> Learn from this
> That things can ordain themselves
> Though they never happened before.
> That these two love each other
> Is obvious to you.
> Listen to some honest advice:
> Smile on their love, and bless
> Siegmund and Sieglinde's union.
> Their sweet joy
> Will reward you for your blessing.

And a moment later, in words that convince us, as so often, that the voice of Wagner is speaking through Wotan

> You want to understand always,
> Only what you are used to:
> My mind is reaching out towards
> Things that have never happened.

In two of the other operas, *Siegfried* and *Parsifal*, Oedipal sexuality is presented and explored. In both of them the central character is so innocent of life that he knows nothing of either sex or fear. He meets a woman whom he does not consciously identify as such. They kiss, and this awakens sexual feeling in him for the first time—and fear with it. His first thought is that this must be his mother. But she tells him that she is not—that his mother is dead and he himself is the cause. Whereupon he cries out in an agony of guilt.

As for *Tristan and Isolde*, I do not think there is a more erotic work in the whole of great art. The salient intellectual influence on it was Schopenhauer, who anticipated Freud in so many startling ways—not only in his central concept of the Will, which foreshadows in its human application the Freudian concept of Libido, but more specifically in his theory of repression.

At one level all the mature Wagner operas except *The Mastersingers* are like animated textbooks of psychoanalysis. While archetypal psycho-sexual situations are being acted out and discussed on the stage at exhaustive length, the orchestra is pouring out a flood of the otherwise inexpressible feelings associated with them. And this is the heart of the matter: it is in the orchestra, as Wagner and everyone since has been aware, that the innermost aspects of the drama are being realized. The most important things in life, namely its psycho-emotional funda-mentals *as inwardly experienced*, are articulated here, as they can never be in words, or on the stage, or in any other outward terms. The Wagnerian orchestra is, to quote Thomas Mann again, 'the kingdom of subliminal knowledge, unknown to the word Up There'.

Wagner knew he was making the orchestra express the world of primitive, unbridled, inchoate feeling below the level of conscious awareness. He stated the theory of it often in his prose writings. A typical example is this: 'In the instruments the primal organs of creation and nature are represented. What they articulate can never be clearly determined or stipulated because they render primal feeling itself, emergent from the chaos of the first creation, when there may even have been no human beings to take it into their hearts. The particular genius of the human voice is quite different from this. It represents the human heart and all its delimitable, individual emotion. Because of this it is circumscribed in character, but also specific and clear. The thing to do now is bring the two elements together—make them one. Set the clear, specific emotion of the human heart, represented by the voice, against the wild primal feelings, with their ungovernable urge towards infinitude, represented by the instruments; it will appease and smooth the violence of those feelings and channel their cross-currents into a single, definite course. Meanwhile the human heart itself, in so far as it absorbs the primal feelings, will be infinitely enlarged and strengthened, and become capable of experiencing with godlike awareness what previously had been a mere inkling of higher things.'

One might put this in Freudian language by saying that the singer's is the voice of the ego while the orchestra is the voice of the id, so that together they expand consciousness beyond all its normal limits into a total self-awareness of which we are otherwise incapable. Wagner knew that he was articulating what in others was repressed, and that therefore there was an abnormal wholeness about both himself and his work. 'Only what is at one within itself is intelligible to feeling. What lacks internal unity, what fails to articulate itself in actual and clear form, baffles feeling and drives it over into thought—that is to say to the imposition of order—while feeling itself is suspended. The artist who addresses himself to feeling must therefore, if he is to persuade it to his ends, be already so at one within himself that he can dispense with the help of his logical apparatus and use instead, but in full consciousness, the infallible receptive powers of unconscious, pure human emotion . . . A man who is still not at one in his own mind about what is really important to him— whose feelings are not as yet focused on an object that will make their expression definite, indeed essential, but who, confronted with an external world of feeble, fortuitous, alien phenomena, is internally divided—such a man is incapable of this sort of expression of emotion.'

One of the many things about Wagner that never cease to astonish is the high degree to which he was conscious of what he was doing. In his books, abominably written though they are, he shows himself a Freudian before Freud—or perhaps rather a Jungian before Jung, for in them he expounds with unprecedented insight the psychic import of myth and of dreams, and the use of symbols, and the function of all these things as alternative languages of unconscious feeling, and hence their unique significance for art. Even in detail, such as the extent to which political and social institutions are illusions, or the partial responsibility of the Christian tradition for man's alienation from his own instinctual life, he anticipated the psychoanalysts. Eighty years before Freud's *Civilization and its Discontents* he expressed its central thesis in his book *Art and Revolution*. In Freud's words 'it is impossible to ignore the extent to which civilization is built up on renunciation of instinctual gratifications, the degree to which the existence of civilization presupposes the non-gratification (suppression, repression or something else?) of powerful instinctual urgencies.' Wagner quite consciously regarded his art as being in revolt against civilization in this sense, a reassertion of hitherto repressed natural feeling. In the somewhat Marx-flavoured idiom characteristic of his political writing at the time, he expressed it as follows: 'In the progress of civilization, so inimical to man, we can at least look forward to this happy consequence: the burdens and constraints it lays on what is natural grow to such gigantic proportions that in the end it builds up in crushed but indestructible nature the pressure necessary to fling them off with a single violent gesture. This whole accumulation of civilization will then have served only to make nature realize its own colossal strength. But the employment of this strength is—revolution. . . . It is the job of art, specifically, to reveal to this social force its own noblest import and to show it its true direction. And it is only on the shoulders of our great social movement that true art can raise itself from its present state of civilized barbarity to its rightful preeminence.'

My central contention, then, is that Wagner's music expresses, as does no other art, repressed and highly charged contents of the psyche, and that this is the reason for its uniquely disturbing effect. To make a Freudian pun, it gets past the Censor. Some people are made to feel by it that they are in touch with the depths of their own personalities for the first time. The feeling is of a wholeness yet unboundedness—hence, I suppose, its frequent comparison with mystical or religious experience. The passionate nature of it, its unwonted depth, and its frequently erotic character also explain why it is like being in love. Most important of all, it is the abandoned utterance of what has been in some way forbidden, and thus presents us with the life of feeling that we all in our heart of hearts would like to live but, in the real world, never can live, a life in which our most passionate desires and their expression are unrestrained—life as it would be if the id could have its way. This is what is so spellbinding about it: it fulfils in art our most heartfelt wishes, which can never be fulfilled in life. This is why it seems to transcend—and to expand the consciousness of its listeners beyond—the bounds of what is possible; why it is so commonly spoken of as a form of wizardry or hypnosis; why even such a writer as Mann is moved to use words like 'magic', 'enchantment', and the rest.

Wagner the man possessed to an extraordinary degree some of the qualities of his music. For instance his life was characterized by the same profound eroticism. The author of the great four-volume biography of him, Ernest Newman, wrote at one point in a different book, *Wagner as Man and Artist*: 'I have given the erotic history of Wagner in such detail not only because of the enormous part the erotic played in his life and in the shaping of his character, but because to know him thoroughly from this side is to have the key to his whole nature.' He was whole in the sense that his music is whole: what is elsewhere repressed was in him lived. Röckel, describing the rehearsals for the first performance of *Tristan*, says: 'He would listen with closed eyes to the artists singing to Bülow's pianoforte accompaniment. If a difficult passage went particularly well he would spring up, embrace or kiss the singer warmly, or out of pure joy stand on his head on the sofa, creep under the piano, jump up on to it, run into the garden and scramble joyously up a tree . . .' Liszt, describing a meeting with Wagner, wrote: 'When he saw me he wept, laughed and ranted for joy for at least a quarter of an hour.' References to him of this kind are numberless. Of the general portraits we have of him the following, from Edouard Schuré, is typical: 'When he showed himself he broke out as a whole like a torrent bursting its dikes. One stood dazzled before that exuberant and protean nature, ardent, personal, excessive in everything, yet marvellously equilibrated by the predominance of a devouring intellect. The frankness and extreme audacity with which he showed his nature, the qualities and defects of which were exhibited without concealment, acted on some people like a charm, while others were repelled by it.'

We can see why the man's personality affected so many of the people who knew him in the same ways as his music affects so many listeners. Some were overwhelmed, and worshipped. Others regarded his almost incredible lack of restraint as shocking or frightening, or mad, or immoral, or in some other way deeply disturbing. Some felt it as a threat to their own personalities, and recoiled, and denounced. Similarly in the music, the same qualities repel as attract: the sensationalism, the eroticism, the sweeping away of inhibition, the enactment of what is taboo. Being put in touch with their own depths may be a uniquely rich and satisfying experience for some people but others are revolted. To these Wagner's music is the voice of the prohibited: it speaks out their forbidden selves. And so they denounce it in moral terms—'dangerous', 'disgusting', 'vulgar', 'excessive', 'self-indulgent', 'sick'.

Sometimes it is the people who come most deeply under the spell who then get most frightened and react most violently. Nietzsche, the supreme Wagnerolater, became the supreme Wagnerphobe. In his last book, *Nietzsche Contra Wagner*, he wrote: 'Apparently you think *all* music . . . must leap out of the wall and shake the listener to his very intestines. Only then do you consider music "effective". But on *whom* are such effects achieved? On those whom a noble artist should never impress: on the mass, on the immature, on the blasé, on the sick, on the idiots, on *Wagnerians!*' And again: '*Parsifal* is a work of perfidy, of vindictiveness, of a secret attempt to poison the presuppositions of life—a *bad* work. . . . I despise everyone who does not experience *Parsifal* as an attempted assassination of basic ethics.' In his biography of Debussy, Edward Lockspeiser wrote: 'It is certain that Debussy's attitude to Wagner was complex, compounded of love and fear, displaying many contradictions and compelling him to lash out with ironic jibes at the object of his admiration.' And another composer, Chausson, once wrote: 'The red spectre of Wagner . . . does not let go of me. I reach the point of detesting him. Then I look through his pages, trying to find hidden vices in him, and I find them.'

Such fascinated detestation is a kind of inverse love. It is revealing that among Nietzsche's last words on the subject were: 'I suppose I know better than anyone the prodigious feats of which Wagner was capable, the fifty worlds of strange ecstasies to which no one else had wings to soar; and as I am alive today and strong enough to turn even the most suspicious and most dangerous things to my own advantage, and thus to grow stronger, I declare Wagner to have been the greatest benefactor of my life.'

If my analysis of the Wagner magic is correct it explains why his work seems to have a special appeal for the emotionally isolated or repressed: Nietzsche; Proust living alone in his cork-lined room; Albert Schweitzer, who turned his back on the Western world to live out his life in Africa; Bernard Shaw, under-sexed and unable to relate to others except through ideas. This is not to mention the composers, for instance Richard Strauss—of whom Lotte Lehmann, who revered him, wrote: 'As a rule he appeared utterly aloof and impersonal, so cold in his reaction to people that they would withdraw instantly and give up any misguided attempt at friendliness'; Mahler and Schoenberg, both of them neurotic and alienated to a degree; the celibate Bruckner. I am not, of course, saying that Wagner appeals to all emotionally deprived people, or only to deprived people, but the words of Mann that I quoted earlier about 'deep and single bliss in the midst of the theatre throngs' touch on something crucial about this art's power: it makes possible a passionate warmth and fullness of emotion without personal relationships.

Not only does the music seem to have a particular appeal to the isolated and the odd; there is actually a long-standing belief that some people are unhinged by it. As long ago as 1891 *The Musical Times* quoted *The Boston Home Journal* as saying: 'Marie Wilt, the soprano who lately committed suicide, once learned the part of Brünnhilde in three weeks. "That finished me", she said shortly before her death. Schnorr died shortly after *Tannhäuser*.[1] Ander went mad studying *Tristan*, and Scaria after *Parsifal* died insane.' Before this is dismissed as fanciful nonsense let it be remembered that Wagner himself feared that something of the sort might be true. He once began a letter to Mathilde Wesendonk with the words:

'Child! This *Tristan* is turning into something *fearful*!

That last act!!!—

I'm afraid the opera will be forbidden—unless the whole thing is turned into a parody by bad production—: only mediocre performances can save me! Completely *good* ones are bound to drive people mad,—I cannot imagine what else could happen . . .'

When Ludwig Schnorr von Carolsfeld, the tenor who sang the first Tristan, died almost immediately afterwards in a delirium of Wagner-worship, the composer felt his work to be responsible. He continued to believe that only strong characters could immerse themselves in it with impunity. He would certainly have agreed that those who despise, deride, or denounce his music are protecting themselves from a real, not an imagined, danger.

People who regard this music as, in a unique way, evil, can use solid arguments to support themselves. First, it is simply true that

[1] This is a mistake—it was *Tristan*.

it speaks with almost overpowering eloquence of incest wishes and unrestrained eroticism, of hatred and malice, spite, anxiety, guilt, isolation, foreboding, concealed menace, the whole dark side of life. Second, there really is serious reason to believe that this may imperil the stability of some people. Third, it is—in the sense discussed earlier—hostile to civilization. This last point constitutes the truthful element in the belief that there is something fascist about it—this and the unbridled violence with which destructive passions are expressed.

The Wagnerian would reply, first, that all these frightening passions are a part of life, and a most important part too, whether in the big world outside or in the privacy of the individual psyche. Without them no depiction of reality is complete, or adequate, or even honest, and any that purports to be is evasive. (This is one of the reasons for *The Ring*'s uniqueness as an attempt to depict the whole of reality in a single work of art.) Second, they form only part of.the content of Wagner's music and not the whole, just as they form part of reality and not the whole. One of the operas, *The Mastersingers*, is all summer, warm and overflowing with human affection and the love of life and art. And some of the best-known music in the others depicts the natural world—the Forest Murmurs, the Fire Music, and so on. Some of it is so pictorial and two-dimensional that one might almost call it poster music. One of the many unique things about Wagner's music, in fact, is the completeness of its range along the inner-reality/outer-reality axis. Third, this music does for some people what psychoanalysis claims to do for others: it releases radioactive material from the depths of the personality and confronts them with it and makes them feel it and live it through. It also relates all this inner feeling harmoniously to an outer reality. It can thus help to put people at one with both their inner selves and the external world; so in a sense it is the most whole-making, the most therapeutic art. Fourth, it is anti-civilized only in the sense in which civilization is the enemy of natural feeling and hence the cause of neurosis. This and the previous point mean that not only is it not 'sick', it is unusually healthy. As for the charge that it is fascist, this is mere guilt by association. Wagner's works have nothing whatever to do with blond Aryans, jackboots, or the gassing of Jews, and to suppose that they have is to accept the perverse interpretation of them propagated by the Nazis. The implications of *The Ring* are the precise opposite of fascism: that the pursuit of power is incompatible with a life of true feeling, and therefore the attainment of it destroys the capacity for love; that because power is inwardly destructive of the people who wield it, it is in the very deepest sense anti-life; that necessary order should rest not on force but on consent and the honouring of agreements; and therefore that the dishonouring of agreements, because it ensures that things can be settled only by force, and therefore will be settled by force, is the most disruptive of crimes.

To some music-lovers Wagner is simply a composer like any other, and to these Wagnerolatry and Wagnerphobia are alike enigmatic. But for the rest of us there is much more to it than that. For us there is something uniquely ambiguous about this music. However beautiful it may be—and many people, including some of the greatest composers since Wagner, have thought it as beautiful as any that has ever been written—it is never only an end in itself, always also a carrier of something else; and it is how we react to the something else that is decisive. To some this music is like the poisoned flowers of the Borgias; to others like requited love. There is no medium in which such differences can be settled, for the realm in which they lie is not merely deeper than words, it is deeper than music.

4. *The Influence of Wagner*

THE most influential poem of our century in any language, *The Waste Land*, contains four quotations from Wagner's operas (two from *Tristan and Isolde* and two from *Götterdämmerung*) and a line from Verlaine's sonnet on Wagner's *Parsifal*. In addition, part of the central section of the poem parallels the first scene of the third act of *Götterdämmerung*, with Thames-daughters substituted for Rhine-daughters. What may well be the most influential of modern novels, those of Joyce, are pervaded with Wagnerian reference. When, in *Ulysses*, Stephen Dedalus cries '*Nothung!*' as he lifts his ashplant to smash a chandelier in a Dublin brothel, we are given not just the cry itself from *The Ring* but a reminder of the fact that the tree in which Nothung had been embedded by Wotan was an ash, and that Wotan's spear, the chief power symbol in *The Ring*, was an ashplant. In the same novel we have the chanting of the blood-brotherhood oath from *Götterdämmerung*. In *Finnegans Wake* we have extensive parallels with *Tristan*, plus a personal reference to Wagner—the 'wagoner' and his 'mudheeldy wheesindonk' are Wagner ('Wagner' means 'wagoner' in German —the English surname most nearly corresponding to it is 'Carter') and Mathilde Wesendonk, with whom he was having an affair at the time he composed *Tristan*.

On all these works the influence of Wagner extends beyond direct quotation, and beyond imagery, to the structure itself, for in them his technique of weaving a seamless fabric out of fragmentary leitmotifs is consciously adapted from music to literature. Most important of all, the use of the interior monologue in the novel originated as an attempt to make words do in fiction what Wagner's orchestra had done in his operas. The novelist who introduced it, Edouard Dujardin (whose *Les Lauriers Sont Coupés*, according to the *Oxford Companion to French Literature*, 'is said to have given James Joyce the idea for the form of *Ulysses*') was founder and editor of the *Revue Wagnérienne*, which existed from 1885 to 1888—concurrently with his writing of the novel, which was published in 1888.

These examples alone are enough to show that Wagner's influence on modern literature is of very great importance. It is wide as well as deep—in one way or another it crops up in the work of most of the outstanding writers since his time. When we remember that during the same period he was the greatest single influence on music and opera, and perhaps on the theatre—and that his influence on a number of leading philosophers, politicians, and even painters has been important—we find ourselves confronted with a *range* of influence on the part of one man for which there is no recent parallel.

The extent to which this has been wilfully ignored is almost incredible. The only explanation I can think of is that Wagner went through a period of such deep unpopularity in the generation before our own that its members were simply not inclined to consider him as an influence on the artists they admired. For instance *The Waste Land* must be the most written-about poem of this century, yet I do not remember coming across any extensive discussion of the Wagnerian elements in it. W. H. Auden esteemed Eliot all his life, knew *The Waste Land* as well as anyone did, and loved opera, but in one of his volumes of essays he tells how it was only a reading of Nietzsche's *The Wagner Case* 'which first taught me to listen to Wagner, about whom I had previously held silly preconceived notions'. Everyone who writes about Wagner is forcibly made aware how widespread these notions are. Prejudice can survive any amount of evidence. However, Auden managed to overcome his prejudices to the point of writing of Wagner that he was 'perhaps the greatest genius that ever lived'.

The time has come to confront the Wagner phenomenon; to

acknowledge, and critically evaluate, his influence on the culture of our age. To do this properly would itself require a book, and one I am not equipped to write. In fact I am not competent to go deeply into the work of even one of the artists concerned, let alone all of them. What I want to do in this chapter is sketch the *extent* of what needs to be considered—mark out on the ground a surface area into which, I hope, others will dig.

The first cultural centre to come under Wagnerian domination was Paris in the late 1880s. 'Writers not only discussed musical subjects, but judged painting, literature, and philosophy from a Wagnerian point of view', Romain Rolland tells us; 'The whole universe was seen and judged in the thought of Bayreuth.' And of the years immediately after, Léon Daudet wrote: 'We studied his characters as if Wotan held the secret of the world and Hans Sachs were the spokesman for free, natural and spontaneous art.' This situation had been building up long before the 1880s. As far back as the 1850s French poets had been writing enthusiastically in the Paris press about Wagner productions they had seen in Germany—Gérard de Nerval about the première of *Lohengrin* in 1850, Gautier about *Tannhäuser* in 1857. The Wagner concerts in Paris in 1860 swept Baudelaire off his feet and made Wagner his ruling passion. The essay he wrote on *Richard Wagner et Tannhäuser* was to provide the Symbolists with their favourite quotations about the interdependence of the arts. (The two greatest French poets of two successive generations each wrote only one essay on a composer, and in each case the composer was Wagner—after Baudelaire came Mallarmé with *Richard Wagner, Rêverie d'un Poète Français*.) The sixties saw the beginnings of Wagnerolatry—first with Baudelaire, then with Villiers and the Gautiers. Théophile Gautier's daughter Judith, who was later to have an affair with Wagner, wrote of those days: 'What this wonderful genius meant to us it would have been difficult even to make clear to those who were not of us—at that time when only a little group of disciples stood by the Master, sticking up for him against the jeers of the masses who failed to comprehend him . . . We had the fanaticism of priests and martyrs, even for the slaying of our adversaries! It would, in fact, have been impossible to convince us that we should not be entirely justified in annihilating all those scoffers blind to the new radiance that was so clear to us.'

Wagner was—both directly and, through Baudelaire, indirectly —the acknowledged progenitor of the Symbolist movement. Its work is pervaded with references to him, many of them idolatrous. What influenced the Symbolists most were not his operas but his prose writings, in which he expounded a new theory of the relationship of the arts to each other, and particularly of poetry to music. But the operas did have their importance. Verlaine's sonnet on *Parsifal* has already been mentioned. References to *Lohengrin* are ubiquitous in the poetry of Laforgue (who was to have such a profound influence on Eliot). And we have this description of the leader of the movement at the Sunday Wagner concerts: 'Sitting there among the other listeners, bent over in an attitude of meditation and concentration, the music made him seem far away; and slowly he took out a pencil from his pocket and solemnly began to write, on a worthless scrap of paper that he hid from sight with elegant modesty. The orchestra dictated and Mallarmé wrote.'

It was not only Symbolist writers, or for that matter only Parisians, who were enthusiastic Wagnerians. There was a Wagner Society in Marseilles, one of whose members was Zola— who wrote to someone in a letter: 'What you call repetitions occur in all my books. This is a literary device that I began by using with some timidity, but have since pushed perhaps to excess. In my view it gives more body to a work, and strengthens its unity. The device is somewhat akin to the motifs of Wagner, and if you will ask some musical friends of yours to explain his use of these, you will understand pretty well my use of the device in literature.' Wagner continued to be a major influence on French writers of all kinds; and in after years extensive references to him were to appear in the work not only of the literary heirs of the Symbolists, like Valéry and Proust, but in writers as different from these as Colette.

A member of the Marseilles Wagner Society at the same time

as Zola was Cézanne, one of whose pictures was called *Overture to Tannhäuser*. Renoir, at his own request, painted a portrait of Wagner, having journeyed from Naples to Sicily in the hope of being allowed to do so. It was in the conversations between these two in Palermo in 1882 that 'Impressionism' was first used as a term applied to music. Gauguin, about to put France and, come to that, Western civilization behind him for ever, wrote to a friend just before leaving for Tahiti: 'I haven't said goodbye to the artists who think as I do. It is enough for me to remember this statement of Wagner . . .' At a lower level of exaltation, Fantin Latour and Redon both, like Aubrey Beardsley in England, produced series of lithographs of scenes from the Wagner operas. Both Degas and Whistler were labelled Wagnerian by their contemporaries. Gustave Doré was one of Wagner's personal friends.

But his biggest influence was, not unnaturally, in the sphere of music. Debussy was so strongly under this influence while writing *Pelléas et Mélisande* that he said in a letter to another Wagner-drunk composer, Chausson, that he kept having to tear up pages of the score because 'the ghost of old Klingsor . . . would appear at the turning of one of the bars'.[1] Both Saint-Saëns and Gounod had become friends of Wagner in the 1860s, and both were to remain permanently and obviously under his musical influence. (After the disastrous reception of *Tannhäuser* in Paris in 1861 Gounod exclaimed: 'I wish God would grant it to me to write a flop like that!') Bizet said of Wagner: 'The charm of his music is unutterable, inexpressible. It is voluptuousness, tenderness, love.' At one performance of *Tristan* at Bayreuth in 1889 Chabrier burst into tears, and Lekeu fainted and had to be carried out. César Franck's music was obviously Wagnerian. Massenet was nick-named 'Mademoiselle Wagner'.

And all this just in France. In the German-speaking world the

---

[1] The name of Klingsor, the evil magician in *Parsifal*, has often been used as a nickname for Wagner. It was used also as a pseudonym by the gifted French poet Tristan Klingsor, who wrote, among other things, the poems set by Ravel in *Shéhérazade*.

first man of genius to come under the Wagner spell was Nietzsche, in the 1870s. In the words of his English biographer and translator, R. J. Hollingdale, Wagner was 'the most powerful and enduring influence upon him—an influence which, despite all his efforts, Nietzsche could not shake off until his dying day . . . Nietzsche regarded his association with Wagner as the greatest event of his life.' His first book, *The Birth of Tragedy*, is dedicated to Wagner and culminates in a hymn of praise to him; his last, *Nietzsche Contra Wagner*, is an anthology of his invective against the composer; and in almost every book between, Wagner is a major presence. Since Nietzsche himself has had an extraordinary influence—on such philosophers as Jaspers, Heidegger, and Sartre, on such poets as Rilke and George, on Thomas Mann, on Bernard Shaw—this also raises the question of what might be called secondary Wagner infection.

Mann and Shaw, as I showed in the last chapter, were Wagnerites on their own account. In his book *Thomas Mann* J. M. Lindsay writes: 'It is almost impossible to overstate Mann's feeling of kinship with Wagner.' For all his ironic detachment Mann rhapsodized about Wagner's operas all his life in a Nietzschean way. A typical example is: 'Marvels, *Wunderwerke* . . . no description better fits these amazing manifestations of art; and to nothing else in the whole history of artistic production are they more applicable—certain of the greatest achievements of architecture, a few Gothic cathedrals, alone excepted . . .' One of his most famous stories, about the death of a creative artist, is called *Death in Venice* (Wagner died in Venice), and the personality of its central character is moulded on the Wagnerolater Mahler. Another of the stories is called *Tristan*. But more even than with Eliot or Joyce, or Zola, the influence of Wagner goes through to the structure itself. Mann specifically thought of his novels as being constructed like Wagner's operas, and as using Wagner's methods. The form of his most ambitious work, *Joseph*, is that of *The Ring* not only in that it is a tetralogy but also in that it raises to its highest level the use of leitmotifs in the novel.

Shaw, too, thought of his most ambitious work, *Back To*

Methuselah, as his *Ring*. In addition he also wrote a book about *The Ring*, called *The Perfect Wagnerite*. But like the Symbolists he was affected most deeply by Wagner's theoretical writings. It was Wagner who had shown, he thought, how a theatre audience's interest and concentration on a sustained exposition of ideas could be maintained by infusing the ideas with passion—what Wagner, we may remember, had called 'the emotionalizing of the intellect'—and he regarded himself as adapting this to prose drama.

Shaw, though a pioneer of Wagnerism in England, was no lone prophet. Bulwer Lytton had written poetry about *Tannhäuser* well back in the composer's lifetime. Swinburne wrote poems about *Lohengrin* and *Tristan and Isolde*, and one called *The Death of Richard Wagner*. There are references to Wagner throughout the novels of George Moore and Charles Morgan, and some quite important ones in Oscar Wilde—Dorian Gray used to sit 'listening in rapt pleasure to *Tannhäuser*, and seeing in the prelude to that great work of art a presentation of the tragedy of his own soul'. An even more famous fictional Wagnerite was Sherlock Holmes. But it was with Shaw first, then Joyce and Eliot, that Wagnerism became *structural* in the work of major writers. Books by novelists as diverse as Ford Madox Ford, Arnold Bennett, Virginia Woolf, E. M. Forster, and Willa Cather contain Wagnerism as a vital ingredient. D. H. Lawrence wrote a whole Wagnerian novel: *The Trespasser*, published in 1912. Its original title was *The Saga of Siegmund*. The heroine, Helena, is learning German because she wants 'to understand Wagner in his own language'. She and the hero, Siegmund, whistle and endlessly discuss bits of Wagner's music. Everything is assimilated by them into a pseudo-Wagnerian world—the Isle of Wight is 'Sieglinde's island', the barking of sheepdogs reminds them of Fafner and Fasolt, the sound of a foghorn is 'the call of the horn across the sea to Tristan' and so on. It is unbelievably bad, but Wagner must have had an enormous impact on Lawrence to make him write it. In fact Richard Aldington, in his book about Lawrence, finds 'the essence of Lawrence's beliefs and teachings' in Wagner's *The Work of Art of the Future*.

As for music itself, little need be added. Liszt, though Wagner's father-in-law, was only a couple of years older than him, and their mutual influence in music is almost impossible to disentangle from the intertwining of their lives. Dvořák 'came under the spell of Wagner', writes Julius Harrison, 'and it took him some years to expunge this influence from his own compositions'. Bruckner was a naïve hero-worshipper. Tchaikovsky acknowledged Wagner's influence, and was himself the most influential of Russian composers. The list could go on. I have already quoted from the letter in which Mahler wrote to his wife, only seven years before his death, that in music there was only Beethoven 'and Richard—and after them, nobody'. Mahler in his turn has been the greatest single influence on such outstanding composers as Britten and Shostakovich. The influence of *The Ring* is obvious in the orchestral writing of Shostakovich's only full-length opera, *Lady Macbeth of Mtensk*, and he once publicly declared: 'I would like to write a Soviet *Ring of the Nibelung*—an operatic tragedy about woman, in which *Lady Macbeth* will be analogous with *Rheingold*.' In his final works—his last symphony, for instance—he took to quoting from Wagner directly.

The young Richard Strauss was nicknamed 'Richard the Second'. Elgar loved only one opera, *Parsifal*, and his masterpiece, *The Dream of Gerontius*, is in every bar the work of a man who loved *Parsifal*. Schoenberg by the age of 25 had seen Wagner's operas between twenty and thirty times each, and the music he wrote at that time was Wagner-sodden. Long afterwards some of the most beautiful music of his pupils was still, in spite of the revolution they had made, thoroughgoingly Wagnerian—for instance some of the songs of Alban Berg. The young Debussy, the young Sibelius, the young Delius, the young Holst, the young Bartók—Wagnerians all. There is only one major figure in music since Wagner who seems never to have come under his influence and that is Stravinsky. And he has told us how his teacher Rimsky-Korsakov, whom he never ceased to revere, 'kept a portrait of Wagner over his desk'.

This chapter has still not covered the ground indicated by its title. I have said nothing of the revolution in stage lighting inaugurated by Adolphe Appia in his designs for Wagner production and now part of the standard technique of Western theatre. I have not attempted to deal with living artists, whose own lasting merit is unpredictable. And I have mentioned only English, French, and German literature. What of all the rest? Are there more Italian writers like D'Annunzio, that lifelong Wagnerian who wrote, like Lawrence, an entirely Wagnerian novel? And are there Lawrences and D'Annunzios in yet other languages? I do not know. And how does one assess the influence of Wagner on the life and work of Wagnerians who were not creative artists, but who may be as important in other fields, and as different, as Schweitzer and Hitler? Again I do not know. But the very incompleteness of what I have written can only mean that the extent of Wagner's influence is greater than I have specified.

Hitler was fond of saying: 'Whoever wants to understand National Socialist Germany must know Wagner.' And although the Nazi representation of Wagner, as of Nietzsche, was a perversion—indeed an *in*version as regards fundamentals—it happened, it is part of history, and it must be included in any consideration of the effect Wagner has had on our time. At the opposite end of the political spectrum Raymond Williams, writing in the *Guardian* in 1966, spoke of 'a particular North Atlantic definition and structure of "the modern" . . . A tradition already . . .'. He was highly critical of that tradition, which he characterized as 'post-liberalism'. It rested, in his view, on certain key books, of which he named eight. And half were in some significant sense Wagnerian: Nietzsche's *The Birth of Tragedy* and *The Genealogy of Morals*, Freud's *Civilization and its Discontents* and Thomas Mann's *Death in Venice*. So it would appear that whoever wants to understand post-liberalism must know Wagner too.

The great misfortune of Wagner's reputation is that he has been blamed for things he was not responsible for—and, in consequence, denied credit that is his due. Many things in modern life that we take for granted were originated by him. I am not thinking only of such things as international music festivals, which impinge on comparatively few people, but of more everyday matters. 'We owe it to Wagner', writes Edward J. Dent in his book *Opera*, 'that the auditorium is darkened as a matter of course during a performance, that the doors are shut and latecomers made to wait outside; we owe it to him that a soft prelude is heard in silence, and applause reserved for the end of an act.' In another part of the same book he writes: 'Wagner invented the steam curtain; steam was released from a row of jets along the line of the footlights, which gave it whatever colour was desired . . . Another Wagnerian innovation was the use of scenery that moved sideways . . . It is entirely to Wagner's initiative that we owe the modern developments of stage machinery.' And elsewhere: 'It was he who started the outlook on orchestral music which has led to the modern idolisation of the star conductor.' Conductors themselves would agree on this last point, and indeed they go further. Sir John Barbirolli once wrote: 'As prime inspirer and founder of the modern school of conducting, I think we can safely point to Wagner, and a survey of his chief disciples, such as Bülow, Richter, Levi, and Mottl, quickly brings us to our own times.'

I cannot begin to claim, then, that I have dealt with all the important aspects of Wagner's influence, or named all the major artists who have come under that influence. But I take it no one is going to maintain that there have been very many others since his time who are *more* important than those I have mentioned—many novelists more important than Proust, Joyce, Lawrence, and Mann; many poets better than Baudelaire and Eliot; many more influential moralists and critics than Nietzsche and Shaw; many better composers than Bruckner, Tchaikovsky, Dvořák, Debussy, Mahler, Strauss, Elgar, and Schoenberg. And if no more than this is agreed it means that Wagner has had a greater influence than any other single artist on the culture of our age.

5. *Wagner in Performance*

'GREAT MUSIC', said Schnabel, 'is music that's better than it can be played.' A simple but eloquent demonstration of this can be got by comparing recordings of the Brahms symphonies as conducted by Toscanini and Bruno Walter. Under Toscanini they are played with an almost demonic ferocity and drive, and are deeply disturbing. Under Walter they have a glowing, autumnal relaxation and warmth, and are deeply consoling. Neither conductor transgresses the letter of the scores, nor their spirit. Yet the sum of what they bring out in their performances could not possibly be combined in a single performance. The acidity and cutting edge of the one preclude the loving embrace of the other. High tension and heartsease are mutually exclusive. Everything each gives us is unquestionably there in the music, but for every element that is realized in performance some other has had to be sacrificed.

All this is true of the other performing arts too. A great play is one that's better than it can be performed, and so is a great opera. Possibly only the operas of Mozart and Wagner are great in this sense.

It means we can get to know great works only by incompatible performances, each of which defines the need for the others. Even the creative artist performing his own work cannot transcend this limitation, so not even his own performances can be 'definitive'. No doubt this is why great composers have given such widely differing performances of their own works. But since we *need* different sorts of performances we should always be open to new approaches to (or perhaps from) great works of art. Our view of them should never become fixed. If any one way of performing an artist's work becomes traditional it impoverishes our conception of it. Or rather, traditions of performance have a value, but they do serious damage if they are allowed to be exclusive.

So the first thing to say about Wagner in performance is that there is no uniquely right way, and no one way is enough. I am not going to put forward a single, unified theory of how it should be done. A producer or conductor or designer has to have a coherent view of any work he is engaged on while he is engaged on it, but he may do a work in different ways at different times in his life with equal success.

However, there are problems of performance peculiar to Wagner, and I want to discuss some of them. The fact that he worked in a composite art-form in which the different elements are more or less successfully fused makes this difficult, because one cannot discuss the elements all at once, yet to consider them separately is to encourage a radically false view. However, if we are to talk about them at all we have to start somewhere; and as, in a way I shall describe later, the original creative germ of Wagner's works was always musical, the best starting point is probably the music.

The acts of Wagner's operas—which are, so to speak, the construction units of his work—are the longest uninterrupted stretches of great music in existence. From curtain-up on *Götterdämmerung* to the end of Act I is about two hours. Act III of *The Mastersingers* is longer. And of course most of the works consist of three acts. One of them consists of four operas. It is a scale that has no parallel elsewhere in music, least of all in the symphonic literature, and it makes these works exceedingly difficult to sustain in performance. Only too easily can they sag and become boring. Seeing to it that they do not makes huge demands on the conductor. The first thing it requires of him is a quite abnormal mastery of architectonics. Not only must he have an assured grasp of these enormous wholes—the whole of each work and the whole of each act—he must also have a command of detail that can relate it to the wholes without sacrificing anything of it, can

show it as interesting, expressive, beautiful in itself and at the
same time a functioning part of the architecture. When this
happens the whole is kept before us in every moment while the
music seems to unfold with inevitable rightness. The great
Wagner conductor is like the builder of bridges who makes a
single soaring arc out of three huge spans over an ebb and flow
that has a life of its own down to the last glancing fleck of spray.
Because of this unique range of demands it has always been the
greatest Wagner conductors who were the greatest conductors—
Richter, Mahler, Toscanini, Furtwängler, Bruno Walter,
Karajan—though they were not always the best conductors of
Bach, or Mozart, or even Beethoven. Many conductors whose
performances of some other composer's work are unsurpassed fall
short when it comes to Wagner because his organic unities elude
them. The best they can give us is one beautiful episode after
another.

It is astounding just how different these works can be under
different conductors. An objective indication of this is provided
by differences in timings. At Bayreuth, where they have kept
complete records, the slowest *Parsifal* during their first hundred
years (1876–1975) was conducted in 1931 by Toscanini (usually
thought of as a fast conductor) and lasted 4 hours and 48 minutes
excluding intervals. The quickest was conducted by Pierre Boulez
in 1967 and lasted 3 hours 38 minutes. These differences break
down as follows: under Toscanini the Prelude and Act I lasted
2 hours 6 minutes, under Boulez 1 hour 35 minutes; Act II under
Toscanini lasted 1 hour 12 minutes, under Boulez 58 minutes;
Act III under Toscanini, 1 hour 30 minutes, under Boulez 1 hour
5 minutes. And although these timings are extreme they are not
eccentric; the other conductors of the work range the whole
gamut between them. And so it is with all the operas. Even the
one-act *Rheingold* reveals differences of well over half an hour; the
fastest, under Heinz Tietjen, is 2 hours 8 minutes, the slowest,
under Knappertsbusch, 2 hours 45 minutes. Often the figures
show the facts to be contrary to a conductor's reputation—
Toscanini's *Tristan*, like his *Parsifal*, was the slowest ever. Often

they show that the impression of a performance which has been formed by the listener is illusory. When I heard the broadcast of Karajan's *Tristan* from Bayreuth in 1952 I thought it was one of the slowest pieces of great conducting I had ever heard, but the figures show him to have taken it faster than all but one other conductor before him.

In all music the impression we get of tempo has little to do with the physical measurement of time and much to do with the inner life of the performance. Beecham was always thought of as a conductor who sent things along at a pretty fast lick, but a comparison of the stop-watch timings of his performances with those of other conductors shows this not to be so. The impression was made by an uncommon buoyancy and spring at speeds that were fairly average. When he conducted *The Mastersingers* at Covent Garden for the first time, in 1913, he was criticized for taking it so much faster than Richter (who had not only studied the work with Wagner but lived with him during its composition and helped him copy out the score, and was therefore regarded as a unique authority) whereupon Beecham produced timings to prove beyond any argument that his performance was *slower* than Richter's. Wagner learnt this truth the hard way. He furnished his early scores with what he later called 'positively eloquent indications of tempo, fixing these with unmistakable precision (so I thought) by means of the metronome. But then whenever I heard about some foolishly wrong tempo in, say, a performance of my *Tannhäuser*, any complaint from me was always met with the defence that my metronome markings had been most scrupulously observed. From this I realized how uncertain the relationship of mathematics to music must be, and not only dispensed with the metronome forthwith but contented myself with only the most general indications of even the main tempo . . .' He came to feel that what more than anything else gives life to a good performance is not even this main tempo but innumerable tiny *modifications* of tempo that could not possibly be indicated by words or figures, but must flow intuitively from the performer. Finding the right tempo in this musical and not mathematical sense of something almost quiveringly alive seemed to him the key to the whole art of conducting: if this was wrong, nothing else could go really right, whereas if this was right the other aspects of performance would tend naturally to fall into place. It came, he believed, from an instinctive feel for the *melos*, the singing inner voice that is at the heart of all music. And his attitude became one of 'if you can't *feel* what the tempo ought to be, and how it ought to change, it's no use my trying to tell you'.

His own performances of his music were very much on the fast side. I once timed all the then available recordings of the Prelude to *The Mastersingers*: the longest lasted ten and a half minutes and the shortest eight and three quarters; yet when Wagner himself conducted it in Mannheim in 1871 it lasted only 'a few seconds more than eight minutes'. On one occasion we find him complaining of a performance of the Overture to *Tannhäuser* that it had lasted twenty minutes, pointing out that under his own baton in Dresden it had lasted twelve. He also complained of a performance of *Rheingold* in Augsburg that it had taken three hours, and reminded everyone that under a conductor coached by himself it had lasted two and a half. Levi, who conducted the first performance of *Parsifal* under Wagner's close personal supervision, took the work faster than three-quarters of the other conductors of the work at Bayreuth during the first century of its existence. Liszt, after conducting the première of *Lohengrin* at Weimar in 1850, received a letter of complaint from Wagner that the performance had taken a full hour too long.

The noisy, ponderous performances with which we are still familiar and which have fixed the popular view of Wagner were opposed to his wishes and to his practice, and were a cause of lifelong complaint from him. When he built his own opera house he designed the whole building round the orchestra pit, putting it in a place that made noisiness impossible. 'The first essential I felt was that the vast musical machine, namely the orchestra, should be hidden. This primary consideration necessitated a complete rearrangement of the auditorium . . .' He not only buried the orchestra under the stage but went on to surround the necessary opening with his famous *Schalldeckel*, a black (and therefore, in the darkness, invisible) curved wooden shield that throws the sound *away* from the audience. The singers confront the audience direct, without any intervening orchestra pit, and their voices fill the auditorium with ease and presence over soft orchestral sound from an unidentifiable source, warm and diffused in quality, every sharp edge removed. The result is very beautiful and quite unlike anywhere else. Bayreuth is frequently said to have the best acoustics in the world. But Rudolf Kempe once complained to me—and no one could call him a noisy conductor—that there were some scenes in which it was simply not possible to get enough volume out into the auditorium: the Ride of the Valkyries, for instance, and Siegfried's Funeral March. When Furtwängler was conducting at Bayreuth in the 1930s he tried to get the *Schalldeckel* removed, but was foiled in the attempt. Richard Strauss, another Bayreuth conductor, expressed a preference for the open pit of the Italian theatre.

Admittedly there is a bloom, a bite, some quality of sensory immediacy missing from the orchestral sound at Bayreuth, and sometimes the singers blur the orchestral detail. But I think the advantages more than compensate for this. For me the question is settled in favour of Bayreuth by its *dramatic* advantages. The visible presence of musicians between us and the stage (the conductor if we are sitting in the stalls, the entire orchestra of a hundred or more if we are in a raised part of the house) tugging at our awareness with their reading lights and ceaseless physical movements, provides us with a human scale against which we cannot help seeing the singers. In Bayreuth there is nothing but the stage to impinge even subliminally on the eye, and by means of positioning, lighting, and adroit use of sets the singers can be made to appear almost any size—a particular asset when the characters of the drama are dwarfs, giants, and gods. Another thing is that in the Italian type of house it is psychologically impossible not to relate the sound of the orchestra to its visible presence there in front of you, and thus to *locate* its sound. It rises up before you like a transparent plane, a plate-glass window between you and the singers which their voices have to penetrate to reach you. In Bayreuth, where the auditorium is plunged into blackness and the orchestral sound begins all around you in the dark, it seems to exist equally in every part of the theatre, and this illusion is maintained after the curtain goes up, not only because there is still no locatable source but also because you are immediately up against the singers. So instead of being like a screen dividing singers and audience it is a common element to both, surrounding and uniting them. It helps to make the audience feel like participants rather than spectators, and to see the singers as characters rather than performers.

It is not to be believed that Wagner put in all that work on those long orchestral inner parts, full as they are of expressive and imaginative detail, intending them not to be heard. And for them to be heard the orchestra must not be too loud; if it is they are submerged, and all we hear is a fat, neutral, homogenized sound. Wagner needs to be played with weight, but also with inner clarity—a combination that few conductors except the greatest seem able to achieve. Another reason why the orchestra must not be loud is that if it is it makes the singers unintelligible. In Wagner the words are important for the same reason as in any other form of drama. I never cease to be amazed by people who say they find a Wagner opera boring and then reveal that they have not the remotest idea what any of the characters has been saying. (What do they expect—surely there can scarcely be any form of drama, or for that matter any spectator, to which the same would not apply?) Over and above this is the fact that, unlike other opera composers, Wagner was working in a composite expressive medium of which the words are an integral part. When they cannot be heard it is not only the coherence of the drama that suffers but that of the artistic medium itself.

This ultimate unity of words and music in Wagner means that the question of performing his works in translation cannot, speaking with the utmost strictness, arise. In other operas, for much of the time, the words are merely a vehicle for the tunes— which is why they can be so silly and repetitious and yet not spoil anything. In consequence, if other words are substituted nothing of artistic importance is even changed, let alone lost. But in Wagner there are times when it would be as true to say that the notes are vehicles for the words as the other way about. I showed on pages 10–11 how the most elaborate series of modulations might be not merely associated with but actually meaningful in terms of the words on which they occur. And not only are every shade of instrumental colour and every harmony then interrelated with a specific word; the very consonants and vowel sounds of the word itself are part of the expressive language, and Wagner deliberately cultivated a verse form that made them so. If, then, the words are changed in Wagner this constitutes not a translation but a transcription. I am not against this even in principle, any more than I am against arranging Haydn symphonies for two pianos, or playing a Brandenburg concerto on whatever instruments happen to be lying around the house. It is not just highly enjoyable but also highly illuminating. But it is no longer the true, original work, and a deep aesthetic incomprehension is involved in insisting that it is.

However, the uncomfortable consequence is that people with no German are barred from a full understanding of Wagner's works. Some jib at this who see it as self-evident that people with no English are barred from a full understanding of Shakespeare's works. The two cases are in some ways comparable. All over the Western world Shakespeare is regarded as one of the tallest giants of art, yet most of the people who take that view do not see or read his plays in the original. So much of what is wonderful about them is independent of the words in which they were written that in translation they can and do constitute experiences among the profoundest that life has to offer. Even so, it cannot be said that nothing is lost in translation. And this is true of Wagner too. So— since most people, even most highly educated people, do not know German—the question arises whether less is lost by seeing the operas in an uncomprehended original than in translation. Seeing them in the original, the audience gets the actual sound that Wagner created but forfeits moment-by-moment understanding of what the characters are saying. On the other hand, if people see them in translation they keep abreast line by line (seldom word by word) with what is being said, but at the cost of its sound. It is a matter for gratitude that we do not, in practice, have to make a choice. We can, and do, have both. (In London, for instance, Wagner is regularly performed in the original at Covent Garden and in translation at the Coliseum. And although most complete recordings of *The Ring* are in German, at least one is in English). This fact, so crucial, renders otiose the sort of running controversy that treats the question (falsely) as an either–or dilemma or (superfluously) as a matter of principle. Wagner-lovers who do not have German *need* both, and they will always, I believe, demand both.

The best translators have a shrewd grasp of the profit-and-loss account involved in translating Wagner's texts, and the best of them all, Andrew Porter, displays a special ingenuity in retaining the same sounds on the most important notes, even when the words in which the sounds occur have different meanings. An example that will illustrate his general method occurs near the end of Act II, scene 1 of *Götterdämmerung*, where Hagen says

Den Ring soll ich haben

which means literally 'I shall have the ring' and Porter translates

That ring shall be Hagen's.

Musically the line is full of foreboding, with a specially baleful expressiveness falling on the prolonged first syllable of '*haben*'. On this, the most significant note in the line, Porter keeps exactly the same vowel sound, and what is more the same consonant to launch it, by bringing in a word that has no equivalent in the original but nevertheless constitutes an acceptable translation of it. On the note immediately before it the vowel in '*ich*' *when sung* has very nearly the same sound as the vowel in 'be'. On the note before that the final consonant is the same. The word before that, which both musically and conceptually carries the second most important stress in the line, is the same in both languages. And by starting with 'That ring' instead of 'The ring' Porter conveys a meaning that in the German is carried by the word order. Translations of this degree of sensitivity come close to minimizing the loss involved in translation, and Porter's in particular have brought new vitality to Wagner's works for English-speaking audiences. But, often, not even he can get round the problems posed by modulation. As explained on pages 10–11, key changes are determined not by the sound of the words but by their sense; and frequently there is no way in which the German can be translated acceptably so that the modulations occur on the words desired.

If I were forced, unrealistically, to nominate an ideal preference for non-German-speakers between Wagner in the original and Wagner in translation I should discriminate between different situations. When an opera is being listened to in recording, the sound has already been abstracted from the rest of the work, which is thus being encountered as if it were sound alone; in that case the original text is to be preferred. This choice is strengthened by the fact that the gramophone-listener usually has both the text and its English translation side by side before him (both are virtually always provided with the records) and also by the fact that he can repeat the whole or any part of the performance as often as he likes, thus getting to know it in an intimacy of detail impossible with live performance. But when the same person sees the same work in the opera house he is confronted with the flesh-and-blood characters being physically active in their visible surroundings, and he has no text to tell him what it is they are saying. What he misses once he misses for ever. In these circumstances nearly all opera-lovers seem to get more out of a work, any work, if they understand what is being said than if they do not. In the special case of Wagner they find that seeing his work in the language in which they themselves live, work, make love, and dream, brings to the surface many treasures of emotional significance that otherwise remain submerged and locked. Even the non-native German-speaker like myself who knows the original texts quite well gets something out of seeing these dramas in the language of his own inner life that he does not get out of seeing them in German.

A recent innovation that attempts to solve some of these problems is that of surtitles. Corresponding to the subtitles on a foreign film, these are line-by-line translations flashed on to a wide shallow screen that runs in a strip above the stage, sometimes across the proscenium arch. Their great drawback is that anyone reading them has to take his eyes off the stage—and the dramatically crucial moments when it is most important to read them are precisely those when the spectator ought least to divert his gaze from the performers. Yet many people like them. In consequence they are highly controversial. Some managements, like that at Covent Garden, have responded by using them for some performances but not all, so that opera-goers have a choice, and this seems to me the wisest policy.

But when all has been said and considered we come back to the raw truth that there is no fully adequate substitute for the original. Because of this, thousands have been moved by their love of Wagner to study German. Those not willing to go so far will have to accept a certain amount of loss.

The fact that words and music interpenetrate in Wagner as intricately as they do needs to inform musical questions of dynamics and tempo. Some otherwise very fine conductors are not as sensitive to this as they should be. Solti used to drown the singers, and the glorious blaze of orchestral sound he put up exhausted them—an exhaustion that could sometimes mar the later stages of a performance; only in more recent years has he mellowed. Böhm often went too fast to allow the singers to give their words full expression, and they sometimes had even to gabble slightly to keep up. Knappertsbusch often took things so slowly that the singers had to extend their vowel sounds beyond the point where they could impart any subtleties of dramatic inflection to the words. I regard the upper and lower limits of acceptable tempo in Wagner as the points beyond which the words can no longer be given full value. But this is not the only consideration. At one time Karajan deliberately sacrificed verbal inflections to evenness of tone, and got the singers to produce sounds of such purity as to have almost no dramatic implications —in effect he used to play the operas as if they were nothing but music, gigantic symphonic poems for voices and orchestra. The results were more beautiful than I believe anyone else can ever have made Wagner sound, and yet a whole dimension of the work was missing. The best Wagner is not the Wagner with the best sound. This music needs to sound less beautiful than it can.

In just the same way Wagner singing needs to be dramatic and musical in equal proportions, and the best Wagner singers are not necessarily those who produce the loveliest sounds. Kirsten Flagstad and Franz Völker, rather like middle-period Karajan, made music so beautiful that one simply gloried in it and forgot about everything else. It is significant that one more often remembers those singers as themselves than in their roles. But it is great *performances* that constitute Wagner singing at its best, and this involves powers of vocal characterization and acting, gifts of psychological and dramatic insight, as well as beautiful singing: my most cherished memories are of Ludwig Weber's Gurnemanz and Gustav Neidlinger's Alberich, of Hans Hotter in his prime as Wotan, and Birgit Nilsson in hers as Brünnhilde, of Gottlob Frick's Hagen, Norman Bailey's Sachs, Derek Hammond Stroud's Beckmesser. In more recent years these have been fully equalled by Kurt Moll's Gurnemanz and Matti Salminen's King Marke. And likewise with conductors. Not until his late recording of *Parsifal* did Karajan's Wagner reach the greatest heights, and by that time he was old and ill and had learnt to live with death; those experiences got into his peformance, so that it was no longer impersonal sound. My other most specially treasured perform- ances include Furtwängler's *Tristan*, Bruno Walter's *Walküre*, Solti's *Ring*, Knappertsbusch's *Parsifal*, Kempe's *Parsifal* and *Mastersingers*, Goodall's *Mastersingers* and *Götterdämmerung*. My greatest regrets are that I never heard Toscanini and that he left only a handful of snippety extracts on the old 78 r.p.m. records. The most knowledgeable Wagnerians I know of, from Ernest Newman down, have tended to agree that the greatest performances they ever heard were those of Toscanini at Bayreuth, which I mentioned earlier in this chapter. De Sabata's Bayreuth performances drew almost as much praise. I regard him as the most exciting conductor I have ever heard in the concert hall; but, alas, I never heard him in the opera house.

Because of the scale of Wagner's works the advent of the long-playing record benefited him proportionately more than any other composer. It put his acts in the same relation to the length of a playing side as symphonic movements had been to the old 78s. During the half-century that the 78 *was* the gramophone record we thought having to turn it over two or three times during a movement a small price to pay for the difference it made to our lives. But symphonies were about the biggest musical forms whose coherence could survive these circumstances. Wagner's works were practically out of the question. As John Culshaw wrote in his book *Ring Resounding*: 'If anyone had tried to put *The Ring* on 78 r.p.m. discs, the complete work would have required something like two hundred and twenty-four sides, or one hundred and twelve records. You would have been interrupted thirty-five times in *Rheingold* and over seventy times in *Götter-dämmerung*; and most of the breaks would have made musical nonsense. Now, with the reasonable latitude provided by modern dubbing techniques, one can accommodate the whole of *Rheingold* on six sides, *Walküre* and *Siegfried* on ten sides each, and *Götterdämmerung* on twelve, making nineteen records for the entire cycle, which has a playing time of over fourteen hours.'

So the long-playing record really made Wagner's works—not his music, but his *works*—available to the gramophone for the first time. And they were outstandingly well served. Each of the four *Ring* operas recorded by John Culshaw for Decca won the Grand Prix du Disque Mondial as the best recording of the year in which it appeared. The first, *Rheingold*, reached the Top Ten in the United States alongside Elvis Presley and Pat Boone, and, what is more, stayed there for several weeks. Who beforehand would have dreamt of such a thing? Of that first complete *Ring* recording, which took nine years to complete, *The Times* critic wrote in 1967: 'It is quite certainly the outstanding single achievement in the annals of gramophone record-making.' The *Götterdämmerung* was for a long time regarded by many people as the best recording ever made of anything—*The Gramophone* called it 'the greatest achievement in gramophone history yet', and *Records and Recording* said 'Nothing like this *Götterdämmerung* has ever before come out of the recording studio'. But what mattered most was the effect all this had on people's appreciation of Wagner. The music critic of *The Financial Times* wrote: 'Not since my student days have I felt so passionately about the *Ring* as after hearing this new *Götterdämmerung*. By the end one is overwhelmed —and questioning all the standards by which one thinks and works and lives.'

6. *Wagner as Music*

TO a well-prepared dish each ingredient is important down to the last pinch of salt. But this is not to say that each of the ingredients is of equal importance—the last pinch of salt is not as important as the meat. Exactly that sort of distinction needs to be made about a synthesis of the arts. To say that opera should be a synthesis of the arts to which each art makes an important contribution is not the same as saying that the synthesis should or even can be one in which all the arts are of equal importance. There has been much confusion on this point, but it is essential to grasp the distinction, because once Wagner had formulated his initial theory he never deviated from the first of these two positions, whereas he began by embracing the second and then abandoned it. His abandonment of it had a profound effect on his work.

In his early and most famous writings he insisted that in the total work of art, which he called the *Gesamtkunstwerk*, the various arts were of equal importance. The next opera he wrote after publishing that view, *Rheingold*, comes as close as anything can to embodying it. But he grew to see it as an ideological position at odds with the realities of the situation, and he moved to the view that because the arts are of widely differing expressive potential— with one of them, music, able to penetrate to the innermost core of things in a way none of the others can—even an ideally realized synthesis would feature some arts more prominently than others, and music would play the star role, would be the most important component of the total expressive medium. He absorbed this changed view into his conscious practice, with the result that after *Rheingold*, music makes up an ever-increasing proportion of the substance of each work, until in the last two, *Götterdämmerung* and *Parsifal*, the orchestra rather than any of the characters is the protagonist. Because he never ceased to believe in the importance of all the other elements in opera, however, most of his early ideas about how they needed to be dovetailed into each other in the compositional working out of a music drama continued to operate, so his later works still exemplify most of them, though there were a few he had to drop as his practice changed.

The catalyst that precipitated this development was, of all surprising things, the philosophy of Schopenhauer, whose masterpiece *The World as Will and Representation* Wagner read in the autumn of 1854. 'His acquaintance with the philosophy of Arthur Schopenhauer was the great event of Wagner's life', writes Thomas Mann. 'There is no doubt that it freed his music from bondage and gave it courage to be itself.' This conclusion has been embraced by every serious student of Wagner's life. The best of his innumerable biographers, Ernest Newman, wrote that Schopenhauer's impact on him was 'the most powerful thing of the kind that his mind had ever known or was ever afterwards to know'. A more recent biographer, John Chancellor, describes Schopenhauer as 'the greatest single influence in Wagner's creative life', and another, Ronald Taylor, tells us of 'the most profound intellectual experience of Wagner's whole life—his encounter with the philosophy of Schopenhauer'. But Schopenhauer was able to act as a catalyst in this extraordinary way only because the need for such a change was already there in Wagner himself.

His own view of the matter came to be that as a young man he had evolved an outlook that was excessively intellectualized and much too rationalistic, and as such at odds with what was going on at the unconscious, intuitive and emotional levels of his personality. And since it was largely from those levels that he created his works of art his development as an artist was giving rise to an increasing disparity between his creative work and his consciously-held views. It was this, he later felt, that had forced him to give up composing for six years, and just stop and get his bearings. The new ideas that he formulated during that period took him along part of the new path he needed to follow, but not all the way. So he was still partially in a state of unresolved inner conflict when he encountered Schopenhauer and discovered a philosophy that articulated—systematically, and on the largest possible scale—the manifold insights of his buried intuitions. It came to him as a revelation. And after an initial resistance he embraced it like a religious conversion. In his autobiography he was later to write: 'For years Schopenhauer's book was never completely out of my mind, and by the following summer I had studied it from cover to cover four times. It had a radical influence on my whole life.'

With his discovery of Schopenhauer most of the things he had believed in his heart but denied with his head seemed to fall into place. In 1856 he wrote in a letter to a friend: 'Seldom has there taken place in the soul of one and the same man so profound a division and estrangement between the intuitive or impulsive part of his nature and his consciously or reasonably formed ideas. For I must confess to have arrived at a clear understanding of my own works of art through the help of another, who has provided me with the reasoned conceptions corresponding to my intuitive principles.' It was not only Schopenhauer's aesthetics that took possession of Wagner's mind but his whole philosophy. The story is one of great fascination, the outstanding example in the whole of our culture of a great philosopher influencing a great artist. I have told it at length elsewhere—in my book *The Philosophy of Schopenhauer*, which contains an appendix on Wagner approaching the length of the present volume—and there is no need to repeat it here. Suffice it to say that—among many doctrines that have nothing to do with the arts—Schopenhauer allotted a privileged role to the arts in the total scheme of things; that he had much to say about each of them that was profound; and that he regarded music as standing aside from the rest as *sui generis*, a super-art, the unique voice in this world of the inner nature of things. When Wagner embraced this doctrine with his whole mind as well as his whole heart it was as if an inhibition had been removed.

In any event, whatever the way was in which Wagner viewed the role of music in his work at this or that stage of his career, we are not bound to agree with him. We take a different view of the work of many a major artist from the one he took himself. Chekhov thought he was writing farces. Beethoven regarded the *Missa Solemnis* as his greatest composition. Michelangelo thought of himself not as a painter but as a sculptor dragooned against his inclinations into painting the Sistine Chapel. We listen with respect to what these great men have to say about themselves and form our own opinions. The accepted name for the mistake of confusing an artist's intention with his achievement is 'the intentional fallacy', and we should no more commit it in Wagner's case than in anyone else's. Whatever he may have had to say, before or after reading Schopenhauer, we are free if that is how it strikes us to regard his music as always having been the most valuable and interesting part of his work. Most opera-goers do this as a matter of course, and always have done: they have never concerned themselves greatly with his ideas. But most significantly of all, I think it can be shown that Wagner would be virtually unknown today if it were not for his music.

When we consider opera—any opera, not just Wagner's—it is clear that the deciding factor in whether a particular work dies or survives is the music *and the music alone*. Most of the operas we know and love have implausible plots or cardboard characters or perfunctory words; many have two of these and some have all three, yet they go on being performed all over the Western world because of their music. Some of the greatest favourites of all have texts that are silly (e.g. *Il Trovatore*) or incoherent (e.g. *Die Zauberflöte*). Works like these have given rise to many of the standard jokes against opera. Opera-lovers enjoy these jokes and often originate them, yet they keep on going back to the works themselves because of the music. As against this, I would challenge anyone to give a counter-example and name an opera whose music is generally held to be worthless yet which goes on being performed for generation after generation because the story or the characters or the words have some special appeal. There is not, I believe, a single one. So the plain truth is that by the end of the twentieth century Wagner's operas would not be being performed at all if it were not for their music. And if that were the case most of us would not have heard of him, for—like Verdi and Puccini, but unlike Mozart and Richard Strauss—he composed scarcely any music of significance apart from his operas. His name would probably be known, if at all, only to musical and cultural historians.

This being so, there is something peculiar about the situation as we have it now. There is this, for a composer uniquely extensive, literature (which goes on being added to perpetually by volumes such as this one) about Wagner's ideas—his ideas about the arts, his revolutionary political ideas, his philosophical ideas, his quasi-religious ideas. Whole books are written about the myths he used, and their derivation. Increasing numbers of us write and lecture about his dramatic forms, and his verse forms, and the peculiar German that he half invented for himself. We write about his life, perhaps the most interesting of any great composer's; and, in spite of the number of already existing biographies, new ones continue to pour out in a never-ending flow. Controversies rage about Wagner and anti-semitism, Wagner and the Nazis, Wagner and German nationalism, Wagner and Nietzsche, Wagner and Shaw, Wagner and vegetarianism, Wagner and sex. Did he or did he not believe in God? Was he or was he not a Christian? International conferences have convened to discuss some of these subjects. And yet none of these questions would have any interest for us, and most of us would not have heard of Wagner, if it were not for his music. Yet about *that* very little has been written, most of it leitmotif labelling and hunting of a kind he dissociated himself from and did everything he could to discourage.

Wagner himself said surprisingly little about the way he composed the music in his works—surprising because he seems to have told us almost everything he could about almost everything else he did. He had, as has been said so often, an obsessive concern with self-explanation and self-justification, and yet this does not seem to have extended to his most important activity. Someone unacquainted with his character might suppose this to have been the one area where he felt fully self-assured and therefore not required to explain himself. But of all human characteristics, reticence was the one most alien to him. If he said so little it can be only that there was little he could say. And this can mean only that the music rose to his pen from levels deeper than anything that even he could verbalize.

From hints, asides, odd remarks, and observations about other things, we get a few scraps of insight that can be put together. Wagner knew that his music had a special power to move and even disturb, and he knew that this had something to do with bringing what had been unconscious to consciousness. In addition, he regarded his true career as an artist to have dated from the time he stopped trying to lead from the head and, instead, put his trust in his intuitions *even when he did not understand them*. This, he tells us, happened for the first time with the composition of *The Flying Dutchman*, his fourth opera. The three he wrote before that he ceased to regard as authentically his. All this points, again, to the same conclusion, that whatever was expressing itself in his work was inaccessible to the conceptualizing faculties of his mind, and was therefore inexpressible in words. This is further reinforced by his often-repeated observation that the initial seed-germ from which each of his works sprang was musical. This seems, at the start each time, to have been an unpindownable feeling, a vague yet insistent intimation of a possible sound-world that did not as yet exist; and only slowly, slowly, and over a long period, and through many intervening stages, did this become concretized into one of his works. To a striking degree, though, each of those works remained a sound-world of its own throughout the whole of the process, distinct and distinguishable from the others, and everything about it would acquire its being *within* that world. There is a *Tristan* world, a *Mastersingers* world, a *Parsifal* world, a world of *The Ring*—they are wholly separate, just as each of Shakespeare's greatest plays is a separate world—and in each case the cosmic dimensions in which the world exists, the space–time unique to it, is musical.

What, then, if we accept all that, about the music itself? Is there anything that *can* usefully be said?

It is common for histories of music, and books of that nature, to pick out two features of Wagner's music for special mention and to say or imply that it is his prowess in these that can largely be held to account for his greatness as a composer: harmony and orchestration. That his mastery of both was consummate is true, but I do not think that either can ever be held to account for greatness. If a non-music-lover were to ask a music-lover: 'Who are generally thought of as the greatest composers?' some such string of names as 'Bach, Handel, Haydn, Mozart, Beethoven, Schubert, Brahms, Wagner, . . .' would have to be forthcoming. But if the same person were to ask, 'Who are thought of as the greatest harmonists among composers?', a reply that might spontaneously be given would be something like: 'Bach, Monteverdi, Palestrina. Schubert. Liszt and Wagner. And of course one mustn't forget Debussy, Mahler or Stravinsky. And Schoenberg . . .' The lists, inevitably overlapping, are far from being the same. And the disparity is much greater in the case of orchestration. The question: 'Who are the supreme orchestrators?' would elicit some such answer as: 'Berlioz, Wagner, Rimsky-Korsakov, Mahler, Ravel, . . .' A composer can be very minor indeed and be a dazzling orchestrator. Respighi is an example. Wagner, wizard of the orchestra though he was, regarded orchestration as something secondary. 'The moment of joy', he once wrote, 'is when the nebulous idea transmitted to my pencil suddenly stands before me, clear and plain. Orchestration, by comparison, is already a public process.' The fact is that most of the supremely great composers are not among the first to spring to mind either as outstanding orchestrators or as outstanding harmonists, though they had as much mastery of both as they needed. The two composers who, I suspect, would be generally regarded as the greatest of all, Mozart and Beethoven, would figure on neither list.

What then does confer the highest reputation on such composers? It is, I suggest, their ability to build wonderful structures out of wonderful materials. The essential gift, that is to say, is twofold: first the power to produce themes that are beautiful and memorable in themselves, and then the power to work these with natural energy and seeming spontaneity into large-scale structures that constitute satisfying aesthetic objects in *themselves*, beautiful in a different sort of way. After Bach and Handel in the development of music this becomes—at its greatest, which I take to involve writing for orchestra—an essentially symphonic mode of composition. It is, indeed, what symphony is centrally about, and from Haydn onwards the greatest composers are, for the most part, the greatest symphonists. Not only did Wagner take this mode of composition out of the concert hall into the theatre and combine it with drama, thereby transforming conventional opera. He did so with a degree of musical genius that is the equal of anyone's, so that his music taken simply by itself, as music, regardless of all its other implications and connections, is some of the most beautiful ever composed.

His themes are of an almost disconcerting pungency and presence. Most of them are unusually concise, only two or three bars long yet so distinctive in personality that they have only glancingly to be hinted at in some remote context and we get the reference at once. This is true even of the shortest of them, which may consist of two chords only (for instance *Ring* themes associated with Mime and Hagen). In *Tristan*, *Götterdämmerung*, and *Parsifal* there are single chords that have been widely used since by other composers yet, whenever used, instantly recall, and are usually intended to recall, their Wagnerian origins. Scarcely anywhere else in music are there to be found themes that are both so short and so forceful. And yet—paradoxically for themes with this strength of character—they seem capable of infinite plasticity in Wagner's hands. He metamorphoses and transmogrifies them through countless incarnations and re-incarnations, always different yet always related, weaving them with seemingly infinite resourcefulness into the largest tapestries in the whole of music. Into this process goes, it is true, a boundless fertility in harmony and orchestration, but his fullest genius is to be found in the free creation of the original material and the free creation of the structures then made out of it—and, when all is said and done, the sheer beauty of the resultant music.

One very obvious characteristic of this music is its nobility. Another is its purposefulness. One is reminded of Wagner's most often-quoted remark about the writing of music: 'The art of composition is the art of transition.' His music is always going from somewhere to somewhere else in a bold and purposeful way. This in turn reminds us of the term he coined for it: endless melody. We get crucial clues about how he wanted it to sound from his observations on conducting, which in the conducting profession itself have been boiled down to the two injunctions: 'Get the tempo right and bring out the tune.' I have examined already Wagner's views on tempo, and we have seen how he conducted his own music in a conspicuously dynamic, ever forward-moving way. As for bringing out the tune, in this context I think that must mean something like this. However polyphonic or chordal a passage may be, if a musician who does not know it says to a colleague who does: 'How does it go?' the other always emits a sequence of sounds in reply. And this can be only a linear series of noises at a certain tempo. It may of course be very simple, but it may involve a lot of leaping about from one 'voice' to another, or a lot of br-r-r-r-r-mming and da-da-da-*da*-ing on the side in order to indicate connecting tissue or harmonic support; and at its most complicated it may require a combination of singing, pom-pom-pomming, clapping, stamping, and all sorts of other noises; but something can always be done to indicate the music. And the plain fact is that music-lovers are constantly doing this sort of thing as a matter of course—it might look a bit silly to a detached bystander, but to the people doing it it is useful, and they take it for granted. Now it is a unique line of sounds such as this, however complicated (or however simple), that is meant by 'the tune' in this context. And what Wagner reiterated was that all music should be conducted in such a way as to bring the tune in this sense to the fore, and to do so in as expressive a way as the material permits. If a hundred or so instruments of widely differing timbres and degrees of penetration are playing simultaneously this is not something that can be left just to happen by itself. Their sound needs balancing, and this is one of the most sensitive parts of a conductor's job. Some great composers create orchestral textures that are specially vulnerable to bad balancing, and therefore bad conducting, and are easily made to sound muddy: Brahms and Elgar are obvious examples. Wagner too knew he was vulnerable in this way, for what his music needs in performance is a combination of weight, inner clarity, energetic forward movement, a 'live wire' intensity and responsiveness to every subtle nuance of tempo change, instrumental phrasing that 'speaks', and a refinement of orchestral balance that achieves a perfect blending of sound while at the same time bringing out the perpetual singing voice that is always there at the heart.

Considered solely as a composer, Wagner was, I have no doubt at all, one of the three or four greatest who has ever lived. But I think also of him—as I do of another in the same category, Mozart—that he was possessed of greatness as a dramatist too, with a genius for understanding the deepest, innermost workings of the human psyche, and that in opera he found or was able to develop a form through which he could express his multiform genius in all these respects at once. The underlying explanation of Wagner's *Gesamtkunstwerk* is not that it was an art-form that combined all the arts but that it was an art-form that combined all Wagner's talents. Ernest Newman puts it the right way round when he says: 'Each of his characters, each of his situations, has been created by the simultaneous functioning within him of a composer's imagination, a dramatist's, a conductor's, a scenic designer's, a mime's. Such a combination had never existed in a single individual before; it has never happened since, and in all probability it will never happen again.' Although Wagner was, it can now go without saying, a many-sided genius, it was lucky for him that his greatest genius of all was for that aspect of his work that matters most, namely the music. But when it comes to the secondary, indeed extraneous activity of talking about his work we—and he—are compelled to take the utterable where we find it. We can hold forth confidently and at length about those aspects of it that can be approached in terms of concepts, and can therefore be verbalized—so we do. We can say very little about the music—so we say little about it.

Does this, in the circumstances, matter? It has unfortunate consequences, because it means that the non-musical aspects of the work come to take a greater share of our preoccupation with it than they should, and this in turn distorts our overall view of it. It tips the balance away from artistic values in the direction of intellectual values. For many people Wagner even comes to be judged by his ideas—and when these are found wanting, his work is declared defective.

The most disfiguring perversions of all that this approach can lead to are some of those indulged in by opera producers. They will seize on the ideas in a Wagner work—or, worse still, ideas extraneous to the work that they regard as nevertheless relevant to it—and structure their staging of it round these. Thus a level that is not fundamental is treated as if it were, and the work is what one might call superficialized. This has happened so often since the 1960s that it can for the present be considered the rule rather than the exception. In the early and middle 1960s, under the influence of post-war Bayreuth, Wagner's operas were treated as if they were, before all else, psycho-dramas. But then came the great wave of left-wing political consciousness associated with the year 1968, since when producers have most characteristically made Wagner's operas vehicles for comment on contemporary and recent history. I have seen *Rheingold* set in a power station on the Rhine with Wotan as a frock-coated, top-hatted, nineteenth-century capitalist in charge of operations. I have seen the spinning chorus in *The Flying Dutchman* played as if set in a rope-making factory under a Stalinesque dictatorship. I have seen the knightly chorus in *Parsifal* dressed as astronauts, and Amfortas wearing a quilted dressing gown of the kind Wagner enjoyed working in. And I have seen innumerable productions that were out-and-out journalism, geared to whatever happened to be going on currently in Vietnam or Latin America or some other part of the news arena.

Producers who turn works of art into vehicles for currently topical ideas and attitudes show that they have no real understanding of what art is. But even to the least objectionable of those who treat Wagner's works as if they were primarily vehicles for social and historical comment I have many objections, of which four are salient. First, it is to treat ideas which can be conceptualized as if they were what is central to a great work of art, and they never are. Second, by doing that, producers ignore the work's genuinely profound aspects, thereby what I have called 'superficializing' it. Third, they treat the actual setting in which Wagner placed his work as irrelevant to it, something that can be dispensed with completely without loss or injury to the rest of the work—a bizarre thing for a stage producer, of all people, to suppose. Fourth, to relate most of Wagner's works to contemporary or recent social settings is to do something that he took enormous pains to preclude: he deliberately set most of his works in a mythical or quasi-mythical world, he goes out of his way to tell us, because their content is universal and therefore *not* to be seen as relating to one particular society. Indeed, for reasons which I explained in Chapter 1, Wagner 'set a low value on political and social content in drama' (see page 13).

Wagner's works need to be staged from the music outwards. It is the music, not any set of ideas, that constitutes their deepest level. This, indeed, is why he called them music dramas—and he came, in the end, to see the music itself as being the ultimate *locus* of the drama. On the face of it this might seem to be at odds with his criticism of traditional opera for treating music as its *raison d'être*, but that is not so. The dramatic content of traditional opera consisted almost wholly of what went on on the stage, and more often than not this had no necessary connection with the music but was merely an excuse for it. What Wagner was saying was that in his work the deepest level on which the dramatic conflicts personified on the stage were lived through and experienced was in the music, so with him the drama was not only on the stage but in the music too, and most importantly in the music. So this was not a case of drama being used as an excuse for, or vehicle for, music: drama remained the end, not the means, but it was no longer seen as something extraneous to the music. The music was now being regarded as its main vehicle. In a marvellous phrase he once said that his operas were 'acts of music made visible'.

It is this making visible of inherently dramatic music that calls into existence the non-musical aspects of Wagner's most mature works. And it is the realization of this process that is the producer's task. However, this very fact means that the score is the most, not the least, important aspect of these works for the producer to know. He cannot leave the conductor to provide the music while he concerns himself separately with stage requirements. And he needs to realize that musical scores of such a length, calibre, complexity and depth take a great deal of getting to know, especially for someone who is not a musician.

However, let us suppose that we have a producer who is already possessed of a secure knowledge of the score when he approaches one of Wagner's works. What is his task? So far in this and the previous chapter I have considered only such aspects of Wagner performance as can be recorded on a gramophone record. However this, even if it is the most important part, is not the whole. We now have to consider the rest, the whole visual side: staging, sets, costumes, lighting, acting, physical characterization, and so on. Like the music, it is on an unparalleled scale. I cannot understand people who say that it does not really matter, for only in fully staged performances do the works become themselves. As we have seen, bringing them to the stage had the effect of precipitating some of the most important developments in the history of the theatre. If Wagner had considered the staging of them as unimportant he could have

promoted concert performances of the music and not wasted
several years of his maturity on the spiritually draining task of
getting a special theatre built. That must have cost the world,
and him, an opera that was never written. And he must have
considered it worth the loss. (There was indeed an opera that for
many years, while at the height of his powers, he pondered deeply
over and nursed a serious intention of writing, yet never did
write. It was to have been called *Die Sieger*, 'The Conquerors',
and to have related to Buddhism in the same sort of way as
Parsifal relates to Christianity. This is the Wagner opera that we
do not have—the one, so to speak, we lost in order that the others
could be realized on the stage in accordance with their
composer's wishes.)

For most of the time in any Wagner work the 'action' consists
in what the characters are experiencing. The amount of action in
a physical sense—as instanced, say, by a stage-fight—is small
indeed, occupying an almost negligible proportion of the whole.
Furthermore, it is striking how inferior, sometimes almost
perfunctory, the music in such scenes often is. Wagner seems to
have little interest in them—it is as if he wants to get through
them as quickly as possible so that he can get back to the real
business of what the characters are feeling, and to the internality,
as against the physical externals, of the situation. This, by
contrast, speaks out in deeply felt and profoundly engaged music.
And that is where the inner voice of all these works lies. So what
the producer has to do is let the music indicate to him bar by bar
how the characters should look and how this should be
changing, what they should be doing, how they should be
moving, their facial expressions, and so on. It should be as if the
music is coming out of them, and out of the stage action as a
whole—as if the staging is the incarnation of the music and of its
perpetually forward-flowing life, its building tensions, its climaxes,
its resolutions, and the rest. But the interrelationships are not of
an unsophisticated one-to-one variety, they are complex and
subtle. Often what characters do is not what they want to do, and
what they say is not what they feel. These disparities also are

expressed in the works. This means that the music needs to appear not to be coming from off the surface of the characters in the way their facial expressions may be, but from deep down in their innards. Their facial expressions, movements, and the rest must always relate organically to the music but they will seldom fully express or reveal it, and sometimes they will appear to contradict it. A deep penetration of the relationship between inner and outer is fundamental to this art, and it is made impossible if the two are presented as being the same—if the characters superficially 'act out' the music. That has the further result of making the stage movement uncannily slow. Emotional deliberation, or absorption, or expansion, are very much slower processes than physical actions—especially violent actions—and since they are what this art is about its dramatic pace, and hence the pulse of the music, are also much slower than action. If the producer makes the mistake of giving the physical action not just a related tempo but the same tempo, the actors are made to move as if they were living in transparent treacle or under water, and the whole thing becomes eerily dreamlike. The key to Wagnerian acting, as to Wagnerian musical performance, lies in finding the right tempo, and that is one that relates organically to the music and yet appears natural and spontaneous.

  In the scores themselves there are sometimes detailed specifications of what Wagner is after. For instance in a wordless passage of fifty-seven bars in Act I of *Walküre* he has written over the first eight: 'For a while Sieglinde stands undecided, deliberating'; and over the next eight: 'then slowly she turns with hesitant steps towards the door'; over the next eleven and a half: 'there she stops again and stands lost in thought, with her face half turned away'; the next six and a half: 'with quiet deliberation she opens the cupboard, fills a drinking horn and then sprinkles some herbs into it from a box'; the next four: 'having done this she looks round to catch the eye of Siegmund, who is watching her all the time'; and over the next two: 'she becomes aware of Hunding watching them, and she starts towards the bedroom'; over the next twelve: 'on the threshold she turns again, looks longingly at

Siegmund and points with her eyes—persistently and with eloquent precision—to a spot on the trunk of the ashtree'; over the next two: 'Hunding starts up and gestures her roughly from the room'; and over the next three: 'with a last glance at Siegmund she disappears into the bedroom and shuts the door behind her'.

Here is the clearest possible indication of the way Wagner wants the acting to relate to his music. And this sort of thing is contained not only in the scores. When he saw his works in rehearsal and performance he naturally wanted to make changes, and he wrote down a lot of revised instructions. The best-known are for *The Flying Dutchman*, which not only give bar-by-bar directions for the acting of some scenes but also change some of the tempi. Of course the trouble with all this is that whereas great nineteenth-century music still sounds great, great nineteenth-century acting can now look ridiculous. I could well believe that if Wagner's instructions were carried out to the letter the results in one or two places (e.g. 'With the *molto più animato* he can scarcely control himself any longer: he sings with fiery, utmost passion; and at the words "*Allmächtiger, durch diese sei's!*" he flings himself on his knees') might be too hammy for modern tastes. But I am not entirely sure. I suspect that a really gifted producer who started out *wanting* to do everything Wagner's way would need to ignore very few of his instructions, and possibly none.

Similarly with his scenery and his stage directions. Whether it would be possible actually to have Fricka arrive on the scene at the beginning of Act II of *Walküre* in 'a chariot drawn by two rams' I do not know; but there are comparatively few such stage directions, and the rest could certainly be carried out by a determined producer. I am not downgrading the producer's contribution; on the contrary, it would take rare talent and imagination to make a success of what I am suggesting. The result would be a scenically spectacular *Ring*, and inevitably also a revelatory one, even if it led us to the conclusion that we can no longer accept Wagner's works when staged in Wagner's way. Of course it might lead us to the conclusion that this is the right way to do them. After all Wagner, like Shakespeare, was not a solitary genius, nor an academic, but a jack of all trades in the working theatre. He was a pro. And one reason why he made his instructions so detailed is that he knew what he was talking about.

INDEX

In the following index, 'Wagner' is abbreviated to 'W.'

Index compiled by Peva Keane